The Greeks and Us

THE GREEKS AND US

*A Comparative Anthropology of
Ancient Greece*

Marcel Detienne

Translated by Janet Lloyd

With a preface by Sir Geoffrey Lloyd

polity

First published in French in 2005 by Éditions Perrin as *Les Grecs et nous*
© Perrin 2005

This English translation © Polity Press, 2007

Polity Press
65 Bridge Street
Cambridge CB2 1UR, UK

Polity Press
350 Main Street
Malden, MA 02148, USA

ISBN-10: 0-7456-3900-3
ISBN-13: 978-07456-3900-0
ISBN-10: 0-7456-3901-1 (pb)
ISBN-13: 978-07456-3901-7 (pb)

Typeset in 11 on 13 pt Berling
by Servis Filmsetting Ltd, Manchester
Printed and bound in India by Replika Press Pvt. Ltd.

For further information on Polity, visit our website: www.polity.co.uk

Ouvrage publié avec le concours du Ministère français chargé de la culture – Centre National du Livre.

Published with the assistance of the French Ministry of Culture – National Centre for the Book.

This book is supported by the French Ministry for Foreign Affairs, as part of the Burgess programme headed for the French Embassy in London by the Institut Français du Royaume-Uni.

institut français

Contents

List of Illustrations   vi
Preface   vii
Foreword   xii

1   Doing Anthropology *with* the Greeks   1

2   From Myth to Mythology: From Native Americans
    to Ancient Greeks   15

3   Transcribing Mythologies: From Japan and
    New Caledonia to the Pontiffs of Rome   41

4   The Wide-Open Mouth of Truth   60

5   'Digging In': From Oedipus of Thebes to
    Modern National Identities   76

6   Comparabilities Viewed from the Vantage
    Point of Politics   101

Afterword   126
Notes and References   131
Names and General Index   153

List of Illustrations

Plates

1 Mount Olympus
2 Epidaurus, the theatre and meeting place
3 Segesta: the temple itself
4 Paestum-Posidonia: abode of Athene
5 Dionysus holding the large drinking vessel
6 Apollo of Veii pictured as a carnivorous god
7 The Trojan Horse in action
8 Hoplites in battle, in phalanx formation
9 Agon, or contest of skill, for the funeral of Patroclus
10 Radiant smile of the Peplos Kore
11 Entranced Maenad
12 Hera of Samos, upright in her temple

Preface

In the early 1960s three scholars based in Paris began to transform the study of Graeco-Roman antiquity: Jean-Pierre Vernant, Pierre Vidal-Naquet and the author of the present work, Marcel Detienne. They brought together at the Centre Louis Gernet a dynamic group of researchers who revolutionized our understanding of Greek myth, Greek tragedy, Greek religion, their social background and early Greek thought in general. Detienne's *The Gardens of Adonis* (Hassocks, 1977: the French original had been published in 1972) was hailed by Lévi-Strauss in France and greeted with glowing reviews by, among others, Edmund Leach in Britain, as a brilliant application of structuralism to Greek mythology. This book examined the structural relations between the myth and festivals of Adonis and those devoted to Demeter, revealing in the process insights into Greek thinking on deities, on sexuality, on the symbolism of plants, foodstuffs and perfumes, thereby totally superseding both the literal-minded accounts of Greek mythology in such handbooks as that of H. J. Rose and the florid speculations about vegetation gods in Frazer's *Golden Bough*.

That book brought Detienne immediate international recognition, although he was already renowned in France for a series of pioneering books on the transition from religion to philosophy and its cultural and economic background. The three books he published in this area (*Homère, Hésiode et Pythagore: Poésie et philosophie dans le pythagorisme ancien*, 1962, *Crise agraire et attitude religieuse chez Hésiode*, 1963, and *De la pensée religieuse à la pensée philosophique: La notion de daimôn dans le pythagorisme ancien*, 1963) culminated in another path-breaking study devoted to the roles and modes of operation of authority figures of different types in archaic Greece. In this he showed the ways in which the categories of poet, seer, king were transformed as those who occupied them jostled for prestige with one another and with the newly emerging figures of the philosopher and the sophist. This book was entitled *Les Maîtres de vérité en Grèce archaïque* of 1967, but it had to wait until 1996 to be translated eventually as *The Masters of Truth in Archaic Greece*.

Close interaction between the leading figures at the Centre Louis Gernet was a feature of their work. The book Detienne wrote with Vernant in 1974, translated in 1978 as *Cunning Intelligence in Greek Culture and Society*, was the fruit of one particularly fruitful collaboration. Once again, conventional views of the development and essential characteristics of Greek rationality were overturned. Where so many earlier studies put the emphasis on the invention of deduction and demonstration, and the bid for certainty, Detienne and Vernant focused on the importance of everything that Odysseus, with his wiles and 'cunning intelligence', stood for, including the ability to win arguments and competitions by fair means, or even by foul (provided you were not found out). It was not syllogistic but non-deductive inference that was the key in most contexts of practical reasoning. This, too, was a work that had a far-reaching influence well beyond the domain of classical studies. It anticipated in several respects the work of scholars such as Carlo Ginzburg and Umberto Eco on sign inference.

There then followed further books by Detienne on Dionysus, on Apollo, on sacrifice, on literacy as well as on mythology. By 1992 he had moved to the USA to take up the Basil L. Gildersleeve Chair of Classics at Johns Hopkins, though he continued for several more years to teach also at the Ecole Pratique des Hautes Etudes at Paris. While he has maintained his earlier interests and continues to publish extensively in the fields I have just mentioned, he has branched out in two new directions in particular, namely the study of historiography and comparative anthropology. In the first area, his *Comparer l'incomparable* (2000) engages in a scathing critique of certain inward-looking, not to say nationalist tendencies in French historiography in particular. France may be 'incomparable', but to focus exclusively on that has often been no more than an excuse to avoid contextualizing its history and its achievements. Worse still are the simplifications involved in representing France's glories as somehow the continuation of those of ancient Greece. In the second field he has undertaken collaborative studies on such themes as polytheism, the belief in 'autochthony', and the foundations of cities. The collection of essays he edited under the title *Qui veut prendre la parole?* in 2003 uncovers the variety of forms that political assemblies have taken in ancient, early modern, and existing societies.

In the present book the reader is treated to an exhilarating overview of Detienne's current thinking on many of the problems to which his extraordinarily fertile scholarly career has been devoted. In the first chapter, 'Doing Anthropology *with* the Greeks', he explains what is distinctive about his own approach. He criticizes here, and indeed throughout the book, those who take the Greeks as 'our' ancestors, who see what is distinctive about European culture, including 'democracy' itself, as having descended more or less directly from ancient Greece and who use such arguments in self-congratulatory mode to trumpet the superiority of Western traditions. Following up the thesis of *Comparer l'incomparable*, he here charges many ancient historians with having a covert, sometimes an open, nationalist agenda. But philologists are also taken to task for their narrow-mindedness. What we need, Detienne argues, is a method that approximates rather to social anthropology (not that he accepts everything that that discipline stands for). He describes his approach as 'comparative' and 'experimental', though the 'experiments' in question are not those of the natural scientist, of course, but rather thought-experiments, the kind in play in the comparisons and contrasts between the beliefs, practices and institutions of different ancient and modern societies across the world.

The effect of this methodology is to redefine many of the problems customarily dealt with by ancient historians in an exclusively Graeco-Roman framework. Greek myth and mythology cannot be studied in isolation from all the other work on myth that has been undertaken in the wake of Lévi-Strauss's magisterial *Mythologiques*. Here, chapter 2 plots the remarkable transformations that have occurred in the study of myth from Lafitau and

Fontenelle in the eighteenth century, through the likes of Tylor, Lang and Frazer, down to the post-structuralists. 'From myth to reason' is a slogan that has repeatedly been invoked, but to see them as simple opposites is deeply flawed. But then what precisely is the positive contribution of 'myth' to the development of abstract thought? And, what happens when myths get turned into mythology, a corpus of myths that become the object of the study of specialists? Chapter 3 cites examples from Japan, Melanesia, Israel and Rome as well as from Greece to analyse the effects of literacy, when myths are written down, illustrating the very different political uses to which they are put and the different regimes of historicity they go to construct.

Chapter 4 returns to some of the themes of *The Masters of Truth*, nuancing Detienne's earlier analysis of the interactions of the different types of intellectual leaders at work in the archaic period, showing how the very use of language, and the mechanisms of the intellect, indeed, changed as different individuals and groups fought to establish their competing claims to deliver the truth. There are, Detienne acknowledges, ruptures and discontinuities in Greek thought, for sure, but they inevitably turn out to be more complex than is generally allowed in grand narratives of the advance of rationality. Chapter 5 then undertakes a scintillating survey of different types of political foundations, with examples ranging from the penal colonies of Australia, through Greece, Rome, Switzerland, to modern France and Serbia. What is it to claim to be autochthonous, born from the land? How are different images of nationhood constructed? Detienne points to the role of what he calls mythideologies in that process. The historians are among those who have a key role in supplying these, so once again nationalisms and historiography are deeply intertwined.

Drawing on the materials from *Qui veut prendre la parole?* chapter 6 undertakes a wide-ranging analysis of the forms of the political institutions that different societies have favoured in decision-taking. We are introduced to the evidence for Cossack assemblies, told about those of the Ochollo of Ethiopia, of the Senofou of the Ivory Coast, and those found in medieval Italian cities, while of course the innovations of the French revolutionaries of 1789 are not forgotten. Those who are used to thinking about citizenship, friendship, justice and equality in purely Western terms will find this opening up of the debate invigorating.

The whole is presented in a prose that in this English version mirrors the sparkling, allusive, elliptical style of the French original remarkably faithfully. I have done no more than sketch the ambitions of the author: but his claims to do anthropology with the Greeks are amply vindicated in an amazing marshalling of evidence from societies ancient and modern. The reader may now be invited to follow Detienne on his breathtaking intellectual odyssey.

Geoffrey Lloyd
Cambridge, March 2006

Foreword

The Greeks and ourselves go back a long way. Clearly, the Greeks are not a run-of-the-mill tribe or ethnic group. At the heart of what historians complacently call 'the history of the West', the Greeks represent a real stake, in the sense of something that may be either won or lost in an enterprise. We should remember that, as André Breton rightly but nonchalantly noted, in both the ancient and the modern world, the Greeks and the Romans 'have always been our occupiers'. If that is so, it is no doubt because, both now and in the past, they have found numerous collaborators. But why Greece? Why the Greeks? Specialists have answered those questions in dozens of languages and in hundreds of books. They say it is because the Greeks were the first to develop a taste for universality, because they invented liberty, philosophy and democracy, because they were the source of 'the very spirit of our Western civilization', and so on.

So much is at stake here that neither anthropologists nor historians can afford to shrug it away. Breton did, it is true; but there was no reason why he should perceive the extent to which the national history of all the provinces of Europe – most of which have largely emigrated to the other side of the Atlantic – emphasized the omnipresence of references to the Greeks and Romans 'among us' – the passive heirs to an increasingly obese West.

Of all the ancient societies, it was the Greeks who spoke and wrote the most, with words and categories that we ourselves have never ceased to use, often without even thinking about it. Between them and us stretches a vast field for experimentation, a nomadic laboratory for comparativists. A 'comparative anthropology of ancient Greece' thus offers a way for us to discover the Greeks not only seen from a distance, but by setting out upon far-reaching explorations, and doing so, initially, purely for the pleasure of discovering new ideas about old questions such as, for example, mythology, democracy and truth! This book constitutes an invitation to introduce ancient societies into the field of a *deliberately experimental comparativism* with the scope to encompass a world that is increasingly appreciative of cultural variability and able to benefit from it when reflecting upon questions that are both general and essential, such as how do politics come to be constructed? How, in between the autochthony of some societies and the nationalism of others, does some kind of identity come to be constructed? How can wisdom or philosophy be extricated from the frames within which they have for so long been hanging on the walls of a Hall of Mirrors?

1

Doing Anthropology *with* the Greeks

'Our history begins with the Greeks.'

Ernest Lavisse

Back in the mists of time, long before the emergence of articulate language, the human race discovered that it possessed the power to imagine itself other than it was. To begin to be outside oneself, to be transported to another world, all that was needed was a powerful smell or an evocative vision caught by a single intoxicated human being. However, to conceive that the spaces 'colonized' by the human race exhibit cultural variation, it would seem that more is required: not only mastery of a rich and complex language but long, sustained, thoughtful observation in circles capable of detecting significant differences. America, dubbed the 'New World' several hundred years ago, presents us with 'the stupifying spectacle of extremely advanced cultures alongside others at an extremely low technological and economic level. Furthermore, those advanced cultures enjoyed but a fleeting existence: each emerged, developed and perished within the space of a few centuries'.[1] In the topmost chamber of a pre-Colombian pyramid, there may perhaps have been a human being, a poet or sage, who did have an inkling that civilizations too are mortal and that others produced concurrently may emerge and be reborn from their own particular cultural productions. Today, the wise men of the United Nations all agree that the development of the human race involves 'cultural freedom', the right to choose one's culture or cultures in a world that is becoming increasingly unified yet recognizes its fundamental diversity.

What I am suggesting is a comparative anthropology of ancient Greece. Perhaps the first thing to do is explain what I mean by 'anthropology' and how I understand 'comparative' in relation both to anthropology and to ancient Greece. The fact that the word 'anthropology' stems from the Greek language does not mean to say that antiquity produced a body of 'knowledge' or discourse, a *logos*, on human beings in general that was peculiar to 'anthropologists' in the same way as, for example, there are *theologoi* or 'theologians', so called because they write about the gods of either their own homelands or those of neighbouring cities.[2] In the fourth century BC, Aristotle remarked that 'anthropologist' was the word applied to a chatterbox, someone with an excessive gift of the gab:[3] a somewhat unpromising start! It was not until the eighteenth century, a little before the time of Immanuel Kant, that in Europe we find the first signs of a body of knowledge called anthropology which, in 1788, was so designated by Kant himself. Subsequently, more importantly, there emerged scholarly societies such as that of the 'Observers of Mankind' (1799), mankind in all its diversity, in the astonishing variety of its 'civil societies' or, as we say nowadays, its 'cultures'. I am using 'culture' in the technical sense that this word was used by Edward B. Tylor. Tylor was one of the great English founders of anthropology-as-a-science that encompassed beliefs, practices, technology, everything that we consider to be covered by morality, law and art, customs, mores, – all that the human beings (of both sexes) who make up a society receive and pass on, transforming it as their creativity and choices dictate, in so far as the latter are accepted by that society.[4]

That was how anthropology began. Now, what about 'comparative anthropology'? The study of cultural diversity in the history of our species must necessarily involve comparison between so many strange cultural phenomena. Anthropology was born comparative. To be sure, it was neither the first nor the only 'discipline' to resort to comparison. Already in the sixteenth century, free-thinking minds in Europe were bold enough to compare different religions. They noted resemblances, drew attention to differences and ventured to raise pertinent questions about the shared common ground and beliefs held to be revealed truths in more than one religion.[5] Beneath the leaden skies of an absolutism at once spiritual and temporal, this was a subversive operation and one that was extremely risky for those who undertook it. To shed light, be it that of a single candle, upon the different ways of reading a book of revelation, of querying the traditional view or of venturing upon an interpretation, was to invent a new comparative history of religions. The admirable blossoming of 'heresies', those remarkable choices made in the springtime of the Reformation, encouraged that invention, albeit without challenging the authority of the book known as the Bible or that of its many clergy.

It was also in the sixteenth century that human beings began to investigate their own species. Henri de la Popelinière and Jean Bodin, those ever-young 'historians', rose at dawn to embark upon a feverish comparison between the mores and customs of the Ancients and the 'Gallic Republic' with those of the New World. At a time when historians had not yet acquired any professional status, the most visionary of them dreamed of taking to the high seas to discover and experience such different and fascinating cultures. Other forms of comparativism were also to emerge, among them the 'reconstructions' of the first quarter of the eighteenth century, some of which were designed to establish a genealogy of the mind, others to situate recognized civilizations on an evolutionary scale. The first ventures into palaeontology, geology, archaeology and biology all practised comparative methods that afforded glimpses of the deep-rooted history of the human species and disclosed the immense richness of cultural phenomena on a global scale.[6]

As soon as anthropology gained recognition as a science – Tylor had called it the 'Science of Civilization' – it set about posing questions of a general nature. These concerned kinship rules, forms of social organization and systems of representation. Between 1860 and 1880 anthropology chose to place in perspective, so as to study them, not only ancient societies, the medieval European past and some, at least, of our contemporary mores and customs, but also primitive civilizations across the world. The first person to be given a professorial chair of Social Anthropology in Europe – indeed, in the world – was the author of *The Golden Bough*, James George Frazer, a Hellenist who had edited and written a scholarly commentary on *The Description of Greece* by Pausanias, the traveller who, under the reign of Hadrian, set off to discover the cults and traditions of Greeks in times past.[7]

But the skies soon darkened as the first 'Great Nations' – France, Germany, and Britain – appeared upon the scene and, concurrently, as history, pompously labelled 'Historical Science', was institutionalized and took to preaching from its professorial pulpit. Once ensconced, it appropriated as its own domain one subject in particular – 'nationhood' – which had first received its political and legal credentials in the 1850s. The task for professional historians on university payrolls was to establish 'scientifically' that all Great Nations depend inherently upon the manner of their genesis.[8] In 1905, the sociologist Emile Durkheim remarked, with some distaste, that it was impossible to analyse 'the obscure, mystic idea' of a 'Nation' scientifically.[9] With pre-1914 foresight (he was, after all, to become the moral conscience of the French motherland), this same scholar argued that 'nationhood' was not at all a good subject for a sociologist since, by reason of its very unique character, it ruled out comparison. Constructive comparison was essential for work on social types in order to pick out their common characteristics, to contrast their respective systems and contexts and then to observe and analyse their invariant features.[10] Around 1870, 'Historical Science' forged a national and exclusive type of history, extolling its incomparability, in both senses of that term: such history was superior to every other kind and, furthermore, could not be viewed comparatively, as was demonstrated by the example of France and Germany, facing each other on either side of the Rhine. The orientation of the discipline of 'Historical Science' could not fail to draw attention to the distance that set it apart from anthropology, which, in contrast, was entirely committed to the exercise of comparison.

Given that my purpose is to set out, in the simplest possible terms, a plan for a comparative anthropology of ancient Greece, we must now see how the Greeks fared after Frazer and his Cambridge associates, who proceeded to merge anthropology with Hellenism.[11] Who were these Greeks? How important were they? In order to determine the places assigned to the ancient Greeks in a field marked out in terms of the tension that existed between a highly nationalistic 'Historical Science' and an anthropology committed to comparativism, it is important to focus upon one essential point that affected the gap that was increasingly to separate the two disciplines. It was in that same nineteenth-century period that an at first insidious, then definitive split appeared, separating societies said to be 'without writing' from societies that were endowed with and soon glorified by writing – writing without which, it was claimed, there could be no 'civilization'.[12]

The cultures newly discovered between the sixteenth and the nineteenth centuries have been grouped together under a variety of headings: primitive societies, savage societies, and societies not yet civilized. When, in 1868 in France, the institution of the Hautes Etudes was created alongside the university, one extremely controversial department gathered under its secular aegis all the known religions, in order to analyse them as different species of one and the same genus. But in 1888, a chair of 'The Religions of Non-civilized Peoples' was created alongside that of 'The Major Religions', the foremost of which was, and still is, Christianity, in particular in its hard-core version, Catholicism. It took many years of ardent struggle to gain recognition of the right to 'Religion' for the group of peoples lacking civilization. It was, I am convinced, when – even before Maurice Leenhardt – this chair was occupied by Marcel Mauss, surrounded by his Africanist, Indianist and Oceanist disciples, that it became the vibrant focus for anthropological thought. Leenhardt's successor, Claude Lévi-Strauss, has told us how, at the suggestion of his listeners from what the French curiously called 'overseas', he changed the name of his chair to 'The Religions of Peoples Without Writing'. 'Without writing' then came to be regarded as the self-evident feature in ethnology, which, in Europe, soon came to be regarded as devoted essentially to societies for the most part ruled by oral tradition and supremely indifferent to writing and other graphic signs.[13]

As the eighteenth century and, a fortiori, the nineteenth saw it, it was impossible to spread civilization among peoples of nature if they remained illiterate: for civilization, writing was indispensable. Written texts constituted the essential mark of historical societies, the kind that made history, about which historians had to write, particularly now that they had become the professional practitioners of a real 'science'. Non-civilized peoples 'without writing'

had to be considered to be likewise 'without history', a fact that
the age of Enlightenment had discovered and that the nineteenth
century then turned into a dogma. The newly born 'Historical
Science' was in no doubt that its proper object was to analyse
written documents, archives and testimonies transmitted by
writing. The task of history was to study and understand civilized
societies whose ancient status could be deduced from readable
written signs. Even today, in the scholarly disciplines of nations,
now mere provinces of a federated Europe, some societies are designated 'for ethnologists', others 'for historians'. Those historians
are ten or fifteen times more numerous and more powerful than
the anthropologists, to whom, nevertheless, in France the Ministry
of so-called National Education generously allots the intellectual
management of some 6,000 of the 6,500 cultures known to us.

In between history on the one hand and anthropology on the
other, where do the Greeks stand? They belong to the group of
ancient peoples, but likewise to that of societies that have also
been classed as archaic, ever since Lewis Morgan compared 'types
of family relationships' among Indian, Greek, Germanic and
Polynesian tribes.[14] The very idea of classifying the Greeks of
Homer and Plato among the 'non-civilized peoples' soon came to
be considered scandalous, not to say unthinkable. Across the board
from Johann (Joachim) Winckelmann to the German Romantics,
Greek philosophy and literature lay at the very heart of whatever
was meant by civilization. So how should we envisage a project
such as a 'Comparative Anthropology of Ancient Greece'? We are
at this point reaching the very nub of the question of a comparative approach. Once historians of the France 'before' France and
the Germany 'before' Germany appeared, nationalism became the
dominant feature in the early form of Historical Science. Even
today, after more than a century of a so-called 'communal'
approach, the history that is taught in the French mother-tongue
remains fundamentally nationalistic. After the First World War,
even Emile Durkheim accepted that 'our [i.e. French] history' had
a universal significance. In the 1980s, Fernand Braudel, a pedigree
historian, took over from Ernest Lavisse and Maurice Barrès. But it
was Lavisse who first realized the important role that a myth of
origins played in founding a history of the nation.

In his *Instructions*, Lavisse declared that what secondary-school pupils need to be taught, without their realizing it, is that 'our history begins with the Greeks'.[15] Our [French] history begins with the Greeks, who invented liberty and democracy and who introduced us to 'the beautiful' and a taste for 'the universal'. We are heirs to the only civilization that has offered the world 'a perfect and as it were ideal expression of justice and liberty'.[16] That is why our history begins – has to begin – with the Greeks. This belief was then compounded by another every bit as powerful: 'The Greeks are not like others'.[17] After all, how could they be, given that they were right at the beginning of our history? Those were two propositions that were essential for the creation of a national mythology that was the sole concern of traditional humanists and historians, all obsessed with nationhood. The major nations of Europe, each in its own way, share the belief that their own histories also – thank goodness – originate in the values of Greece and that *their* Greeks are, naturally, beyond compare. Anthropologists of Greece who had had the effrontery to compare the mythology and thought of the Greeks with the risqué stories of the savages of America and Polynesia were promptly marginalized, if not well and truly excommunicated.[18] Today, as no doubt tomorrow too, it is commonly accepted among Hellenists and antiquarians, both in Europe and in the United States of America, that Greece remains the birthplace of the West and of all the values that conservatives the world over defend with equal vigour. The Greeks, who were once scattered in tribes throughout a thousand and one motley cities, have become *our* Greeks: it is in them that our Western autochthony must be founded and rooted.

By thus appropriating the Greeks, the nationalistic historians of the West seem to have definitively removed the ancient societies of Greece from the domain of the scholarship of anthropologists who, in Europe, are few enough anyway and who, in the New World, are woefully inadequately informed of what is at stake.[19] For in truth much certainly is at stake for comparative studies in our multicultural world and for the kind of anthropological thought that challenges both incomparability and the West's declared claim that it has always been exceptional, on account of its purely Greek values.

Paradoxically enough, the impression that the Greeks are our closest neighbours, which some of our 'humanists' may nurture, is based upon common issues and categories, many of which are precisely those upon which early comparative anthropology decided to focus. As I have noted above, the founders of anthropology, while being imbued with the very best kind of Englishness, laid the basis of the 'Science of Civilization' by proceeding from descriptions of the aboriginal Australians to the treatises of Plutarch, and from the mythology of the Iroquois to reflections on myth by Xenophanes, the philosopher of Colophon. Out of this dialogue that the young anthropologists of the nineteenth century set up between ancient Greeks and primitive peoples emerged major issues for the new discipline and excellent questions on the basis of which we can, as I hope to show, involve ourselves in comparative anthropology *with* the Greeks, possibly adopting a new methodology.

Let me begin by listing a few of those issues, briefly indicating why they are relevant today. The first is myth, along with mythology and 'mythical thought'. Then come the relations between orality and writing. Next, those between philosophy and wisdom, and the question of truth. And finally, the origin of politics and the invention of 'democracy'.

One early line of thought about the nature of myths and their meaning in the history of the human race unfolded, with Fontenelle and Lafitau, in the eighteenth century, around the 'fable' of the Greeks and the Americans. Today, as in the past, debates on 'primitive thought' or 'mythical thought' are inseparably linked with the status of mythology as recognized among the ancient Greeks.[20] Whether they appear as mutants or as mediators, the Greeks of antiquity seem to present in their culture, or at least in that of Homer and the eighth century, a state of civilization midway between forms of orality and the already diversified practices of writing. Should those early Greeks be classified among the societies 'with' writing or those 'without'? For Historical Science and the tribe of historians as a whole, that is an important question and much research has been devoted to a comparison between different types of oral poetry and oral practices generally. Meanwhile, anthropologists working with certain doughty Hellenists have successfully explored and compared the effects of the introduction of writing in a wide range of different types of society in which new subjects for intellectual consideration can be seen to have emerged.[21] In the land of Pythagoras and Parmenides, philosophy and wisdom were always considered to be indigenous. The invention of philosophy was absolutely and emphatically claimed by archaic Greece, while ancient China was allowed a monopoly over wisdom. Clearly, the Seven Sages were never consulted on the matter, and comparative studies set out to qualify such a simple-minded dichotomy by dint of analyses of a series of microconfigurations, encompassing, for instance, 'places and names allotted to truth' in both 'philosophy' and other forms of knowledge.[22]

Finally, there is politics (with or without a capital P) that seems to be an exclusively Greek, if not Athenian, discovery and one that appears indispensable to any enquiry into social systems in Africa and India and equally so to any attempts to understand the various other forms of power that Aristotle and other excellent observers of the human race identified. In the United States of America, as in Europe, it is commonly said that it was in Greece that Democracy (with a capital D) fell to earth from the heavens. But among entrenched scholars and the ignorant alike, far less is known of what we might learn from a comparative approach to practices that produce 'something akin to politics' in all the hundreds of small societies – communities, cities, chiefdoms, ethnic groups, tribes – that are scattered throughout the world.[23]

It would not be hard to add further themes to those mentioned above: for example, history (*historia*), in the Greek Herodotean sense of an 'enquiry' that produces historicity and its attendant forms of historiography. This constitutes a field of strategic research into a type of anthropology *with* (that is to say 'using') the Greeks that should call into question the assumptions of a historiography trapped by Occidentalism as much as by the nationalistic framework of early 'Historical Science'.[24] Linked closely to the theme of history is that of autochthony, equally Greek but as yet hardly touched, despite the fact that it leads directly[25] to a number of ways of 'carving out a territory', one of which, very familiar to our twenty-first-century contemporaries, is known as claiming a 'national identity'. As is shown by the above list of themes, comparative anthropology focuses on problems. It is wary of intuitive approaches and impressionistic comparisons and challenges commonplace generalizations. So it is important to determine precisely what *approach* to adopt, what *method* to follow, as we say, *after* having tried to map out some kind of orientation.

The comparativism that I am championing and hope to illustrate in this book is a fundamentally *joint* operation between ethnologists and historians. It is a comparativism that is both *experimental* and *constructive*.[26] In accordance with the customary demarcation lines between disciplines, anthropologists and historians have become accustomed to living and thinking in separate worlds: worlds separated by prejudices as futile as that inherited from the nineteenth century which set societies 'without' history apart from those 'with'. Nothing but intellectual laziness is preventing comparativism from developing between historians and anthropologists working together. After all, is it not up to them, to promote between them an understanding of all the human societies and all the cultures in the world, across both time and space?

As regards methodology, I should stress how important it is for a comparativist to be at once singular and plural. But what kind of a comparativist do I have in mind? One who takes shape thanks to an intellectual network woven to include a number of ethnologist historians and historian ethnologists. The enterprise – and that is certainly the word for it – may be undertaken by a couple of scholars working together, one a historian, the other an anthropologist, provided each shares the intellectual curiosity and skills of the other. We should, then, *work together*, in groups of two or four, but each of us must believe that it is as important to be sustained by the knowledge and questions of our partners as it is to analyse in depth the society for which each of us, either as an anthropologist or as a historian, has chosen to become a 'professional' interpreter. There can be no doubt that a regular attendance at seminars disposes people to think together and out loud. Working together in a mixed group comprising both ethnologists and historians, well, you might ask, what is so new about that?

It has been ages since ethnologists and historians met up and began to move forward in convoy. Travelling in convoy certainly implies keeping an eye on one another as you navigate. You observe your companions, rub shoulders with them, sometimes borrowing a subject (immediately dubbed 'a new subject') or an expression that provokes an agreeably exciting feeling that you are thinking in a new way. The way that anthropology stands back from its object and views it from afar is both unsettling and attractive to history, particularly if, perchance, glancing in the mirror one morning, the latter decides that it looks somewhat jaded, less beautiful, a touch more ponderous than it used to. The two disciplines usually enjoy a flirtation, but seldom a full-blown relationship. Their more serious practitioners soon return to their own affairs. Historians make the most of the opportunity to reassert their preference for comparisons among themselves, with their close and longstanding neighbours. The wiser among them do acknowledge a certain weakness for fine similarities and analogies. But there is no getting around the fact that the fervent advice of the entire establishment – clergy, academies and all the institutions that really count – is that history should not take ethnology as its bedfellow. Ethnology is, of course, alluring, but really not from the same social bracket. Besides, rumour has it that it does not have much of a future: out of work today; and tomorrow, without the necessary official credentials, who knows? We have been warned by our elders: this is not the way to end up with a seat in the Academy.

Nevertheless, I persevere: can comparativism be a profession? And the answer is 'Yes', one *can* be a professional comparativist, even an *experimental* and *constructive* one. Experimental? In what sense? As historians and ethnologists working together, we can pool a wealth of knowledge about hundreds, even thousands of different cultures and societies ranging across both space and time.[27] I am fully convinced that our common task is to analyse human societies and to understand as many of their cultural products as possible. Why ever not 'experiment' on the basis of 'earlier experiments', given that it is not only possible to do so but, furthermore, acts as an excellent stimulus to the intellectual activity of historians and anthropologists alike? It involves working together, freely, for years, moving from one society to another, always in the indispensable company of experts, specialists in each particular terrain. Without the active commitment of a collaborating group, a little laboratory of ethnologists and historians on the move, a group constantly renewed, there can be no comparativism that is at once *experimental* and constructive.

There seems to me to be little point in arguing about whether it is more profitable to compare 'what is close' or 'what is distant'.[28] The one does not exclude the other. All the same, I do believe that comparativism is more vibrant and more stimulating if ethnologists and historians are able and willing to lend an ear to dissonances that at first seem 'incomparable', and to put them in perspective. By dissonance I mean, for example, a case where a society appears to make no room for an institution or configuration that our kind of common sense regards as normal and natural, or where a system of thought encountered elsewhere does not appear to offer any obvious category.

Once a historian or an ethnologist, trained to work on some local and precise problem, reaches the conclusion that our notion of what 'personality' is constitutes a rather unusual idea within the framework of all the cultures in the world, he really is beginning to think as an anthropologist,[29] or is at least taking the first steps in that direction. The next step might entail the discovery that 'the better to analyse the symbolic forms of a foreign culture, you have to delve into the *cast of mind* of another people'.[30]

Here we come to the nub of the matter. To experiment and then to construct what it is that ethnologists and historians are together going to compare, you have to pick out a concept or category. It should be neither too parochial and specific nor too general and comprehensive. An example, to which I shall be returning at length, may show what I mean by 'to experiment' and 'to be constructive'. In an enquiry undertaken twenty or so years ago, I/we – a small group of Hellenists and Africanists – wondered how we could produce a comparative analysis of an action as common and as interesting as that of 'founding'.[31] The first phase of experimentation involves discovering societies or cultural groups that provide models of types and practices of 'foundation'. How does one set about 'founding' in Vedic India or in the societies of West Africa? In all likelihood, in different and contrasting ways. All the members of the little group of researchers thereupon feel free to branch out from the societies closest to their own chosen terrains and to go off in search of cultures and societies that are in principle 'untouchable' for any self-respecting historian or strictly correct ethnologist trained never to wander from his/her particular cultural area or his/her particular adopted community.

That is the first move to make. The second comes hard on its heels, once the group members begin to venture further afield and travel from one culture to another, frequently between ones that are separated by vast distances. This is the surest way to discover a society in which there seems to be no equivalent of 'founding' or 'foundation'. The local experts are categorical: in the society of which they are the historians or ethnologists, 'there is no such thing as founding': there is simply restoration, ceaseless restoration. What is discovered seems to be a perfect dissonance: a category that seemed commonsensical more or less everywhere begins to waver and soon crumbles away. The comparativist/comparativists, now on the alert, immediately begin to wonder: what is it that we ascribe to 'founding' that makes it a very particular way of doing something that amounts to not just 'inhabiting' or 'being in a certain space', but 'establishing a territory'? 'Establishing a territory' may involve certain forms of autochthony of a native or aboriginal character and also ways of inhabiting a particular place after arriving from outside or elsewhere.

'Founding' was not a bad point of entry. 'Establishing a territory' was an even better one – above all, a better way to begin to *construct* what can be compared. What, after all, is the meaning that we ascribe to 'founding', to 'being autochthonous' or 'aboriginal'? If we set about analysing a series of very different ways of 'establishing a territory', we begin to pose questions that soon branch out in two main directions: on the one hand, what is the meaning of to begin, to inaugurate, to historicize, to historialize? On the other, what does it mean to be born in a particular place, to be a native, to be called indigenous, to have or not to have roots? And what is a place? What is a site? The comparativist/comparativists, alerted by one or several dissonances, then proceeds/proceed to coin a new category or set of concepts. They move constantly from one culture or society to another if these seem of a kind to make the *conceptual* elements that have been discovered productive. They try to see how known cultural systems *react* not only to the initial category that was selected as a touchstone, but also to the series of questions that now arise and the conceptual elements that gradually come to light.

So 'our history' does not begin with the Greeks. It is infinitely vaster than a single territory such as France or England and the beliefs of its accredited authorities. Rather, let us do anthropology *with* the Greeks. That is the invitation to a voyage offered by this book, which aims to discover at least some aspects of the art of constructing comparabilities.

2

From Myth to Mythology:

From Native Americans to Ancient Greeks

To us, nothing seems more Greek than mythology, both the word and mythology itself.[1] Despite a few patches of chiaroscuro, a long cultural and figurative tradition creates for us an impression of pellucid familiarity with the stories of Greek mythology. For close on two centuries already, mythology and the nature of myth have constituted one of the major subjects of the reflections of both anthropologists and philosophers.

Today in the West, thinking about myth involves, first, recognizing and to some extent succumbing to the fascination that mythology and its imaginary representations continue, as always, to exert upon us and upon the history of our most intimate thinking. This fascination stems from an uninterrupted reading, enriched by every analogy presented by the course of history ever since the earliest Greek beginnings. The word 'myth', in itself, is in no way deceptive. But when its semantic shifts are carefully studied, its transparency becomes somewhat clouded. For this reason, the best approach to adopt seems to be a reflexive one that does not deflect the analysis of myths from its object but firmly encourages it to take account of the complexity of the material.

On fables and religion in the eighteenth century

In the early eighteenth century, mythology and the nature of mythology fuelled a debate that involved the Americans and the Greeks – or, to be more precise, the first inhabitants of the New

World and the people of early antiquity. The debate, prompted as early as the sixteenth century by contact with Native Americans, intensified in 1724, the year that saw the publication of works by both Fontenelle and Lafitau. Fontenelle's was a pamphlet, *On the Origin of Fables*, while Lafitau's work concerned *The Mores of the Savages of America compared to the Mores of the Earliest Times*. The resemblance between the form and content of the stories of the Iroquois and those of Hesiod's Greeks provided the basis for a kind of comparative mythology. Everywhere and always, it seemed, people invent fables, but to what kind of thought do these belong? The originality of Lafitau lay in showing the strange 'conformity' between the mores and customs of the Native Americans and those of the ancient Greeks – a conformity detectable in their practices of abstinence, their modes of initiation, their sacrificial rites, and even the shape of their huts, all of which indicated a 'collection of duties' and a 'civil religion' in which cult practices were organized as a public service, useful to society. Right from the earliest days, the great body of customs that extends from the Ancient to the New World bears the imprints of religion: hieroglyphics, symbols and emblems, mysterious figures designed to teach the secrets of initiations and mysteries. Lafitau discovered a kind of religion long antedating Christianity and the Bible, that of early paganism, upon which the 'conformity' between the Greeks and the Native Americans was founded. But what was to be made of the fables and mythology of the Native Americans and those of the ancient Greeks? In contrast to religion, mythology proliferates with ignorance, is fuelled by passions, makes its appearance when a cult begins to fall apart. Fables emerged out of the decadence of that early paganism, full of carnal notions as gross and ridiculous among the Greeks as in the Iroquois societies: notions that constituted a gangrene in the fine 'collection of duties' that the representatives of that original world were recognized to possess.

While Lafitau, a Jesuit, conceded to primitive humanity the virtues of a religion antedating Christianity, Fontenelle, a man of the Enlightenment who was also curious about this strange product of the human spirit, could see in its fables and mythology nothing but a common ignorance that was shared by both the

Ancient World and the New World in their earliest days. In those uncouth centuries that did not yet speak the language of reason, human beings, wanting to explain phenomena and the world, invented fables. In their ignorance, they could make out nothing but prodigies and were thus led to tell stories about chimeras and strange, dreamlike figures. Perhaps those barbaric and infantile societies – whether Greek, Iroquois, Kaffir or Lapp – were engaged in a primitive kind of philosophic activity. But Fontenelle could distinguish in it nothing but stammerings – foolishness that, as he saw it, made the grave mistake of 'turning into religion', among most of those peoples at least.

While Lafitau thought that religion came first and was then degraded into fables, the author of *On the Origin of Fables* chose to regard all those absurd and senseless stories as the first forms of what would later become religion, for the ancients and the barbarians of both yesterday and today. To the credit of the Greeks and the Romans, Fontenelle declared that, for them, fables also became a source of pleasure, initially for the ear and later – thanks to the images conceived and produced by painters and sculptors – also for the eye. For this enlightened mind, that was enough to justify the effort that he and his contemporaries had made to trace the mythological subjects of so many pictures and also the stories invented by the ancients, stories that constituted the sources of so many literary works.

Myth, language and comparison

In early eighteenth-century France, mythology thus found neither a place nor an image that made it distinctive. Although they were in agreement as to the erroneous and vain nature of fables, neither Fontenelle nor Lafitau was in a position to generate any real comparative mythology. Even then, in their view, myth and mythology surely had to be apprehended in relation to the subject that, between the eighteenth and the nineteenth centuries, commanded universal attention – that is to say religion, whether this was regarded as a massive, general Christian institution or, by the sixteenth century, a subject that raised overt problems, as shown by the religious wars and the earliest conflicting interpretations of

Christianity. It was only thanks to new ways of thinking about language that, in the nineteenth century, an approach to mythology as such was initiated. In the early years of the nineteenth century a whole series of discoveries and advances modified the status of language: these included the publication of the *Vedas* and the appearance of Sanskrit philology; the first studies, in French and English, of the *Gathas* and the *Avesta*; and in 1816, in Germany, the publication of the first elements of a comparative grammar by Franz Bopp. In the wake of the natural sciences and with the introduction of linguistics, comparison became a paradigm, a theoretical model that the new science of language would extend to other areas, including those of myth and mythology.

The connection between myth and language was made through phonetics and the study of sounds. Sounds, syllables and roots, liberated from the letters that happened to transcribe them, are so many formal elements, whose modifications are governed by the laws of phonetics. Meanwhile, there emerged the idea of language as the speech of the people, the sonorous shifts of which testify to the constant activity that seems inseparable from movement and history. A speech of the people and the nation was thus discovered. At a deeper level, at the origins of the human race revealed by the Sanskrit of the *Vedas*, primitive language seemed to consist of both speech and song. It could cope with neither abstraction nor deceit. That primitive language, which antedated civilized languages, possessed the energy and grandeur of original, faithful expression. Within this new space of sounds the myths of the ancients became the object of scholarship that mobilized comparison between these stories of ancient civilizations and those of the primitive societies in which, a little later, the founders of anthropology took an interest.

Friedrich-Max Müller (1823–1900) was to found a veritable school of comparative mythology. In his book *The Science of Language*, he set out a stratigraphy of human speech, in which he distinguished three phases: thematic, dialectical and mythopoietic. In the first phase, terms were forged to express the most necessary ideas. In the second, the grammatical system acquired its specific characteristics once and for all. The mythopoietic phase saw the appearance of mythical discourse that was not at all a conscious product of language. As Müller saw it, just as grammatical structures silently took shape in the abysses of language, so too myths first appeared like bubbles bursting at the surface of the words and phrases that rose to the lips of the earliest human beings. At the dawn of history, a human being possessed the faculty to pronounce words that gave direct expression to the essence of the objects perceived by the senses. Things awakened within the individual sounds that materialized as roots and engendered phonetic types on the basis of which a body of language was progressively formed. However, the human mind did not long retain the privilege of 'giving articulated expression to concepts produced by reason'. Once human beings ceased to 'resonate' before the world, a sickness invaded language. Soon the human race would become a victim of the illusions produced by words.

The earliest language possessed a kind of energy that allowed the earliest human beings to apprehend the meaning of words such as 'night and day' or 'morning and evening' and, at the same time, to conceive of them as powerful beings marked by a particular sexual nature. However, as soon as the primitive essence of the words 'night and day' or the names 'Night and Day' changed and became clouded, mythical figures swarmed into the field of representation.

The human beings of the third phase found themselves to be assailed by the illusions of a language invaded by the strange and disconcerting discourse of myths. For Müller, mythology – in the first place that of the ancients – was a sickness in language. Linguists, now acting as clinicians, detected in the fables and stories of mythology a pathological form, not so much of thought, but of language and the excess of meaning from which it suffered at one point in its development. At a stroke, the paths of interpretation were marked out: all that was necessary was to diagnose behind the major narratives of mythology the forms taken by the spectacle of nature that impressed the earliest human beings. Thus, whether in India or in Greece or elsewhere, myths reflect a tragedy of nature in which a sense of storms and tempests alternates with impressions produced by the spectacle of sunshine and light.

Mythical thought: the foundation of anthropology

The 'science of language' that turned into comparative mythology took mythical narratives apart and disintegrated them, only too happy to burst the bubbles that had once risen to the surface of the words and sentences of human beings now long forgotten. Comparative mythology was partly motivated by the same sense of scandal that seems to have been felt by the new observers of humankind who, in the 1880s, turned into anthropologists. They were scandalized by the obscene and odious discourse purveyed by the mythology of the Greeks, which told of the emasculation of Ouranos and the death of Dionysus, cut into pieces and barbecued on a spit. All those who devoted themselves to the 'science of myths' or 'comparative mythology' – Edward Burnett Tylor (1832–1917), Adalbert Kuhn (1812–81), Andrew Lang (1844–1912), Paul Decharme (1839–1905) – concurred as to the urgency of the task of explaining, not the wonderful stories produced by those early human beings, but the 'savage and meaningless' tales about the appearance of death or of the sun, and the 'monstrous and ridiculous' adventures involving incest, murder and cannibalism that befell the gods. Between 1850 and 1890, from Oxford to Berlin and from London to Paris, the 'science of myths' was established on the basis of the common opinion that bodies of myth were full of notions of a 'revoltingly immoral nature'. That was certainly true right across the world, but also and above all in so many ancient societies that appeared to have attained a high degree of civilization. Beneath the surface, the ancient Greek and the Vedic priest were obsessively linked to the 'savage' and the Iroquois.

But the strategy adopted by Tylor was quite unlike that of Müller. The earliest concept of anthropology is reflected in the proposed aim, taken over from Lafitau and Fontenelle, of revealing the 'astonishing conformity between the fables of the Americans and those of the Greeks'. Now the comparisons that were prompted by the scandalous nature of myth were extended to include the whole body of stories told among Australian Aborigines, Native Americans, Bushmen, and also the representatives of ancient societies. Stories that an anthropologist could now bring back from his missions in distant places could not be explained away as resulting from a misunderstanding of a few particular expressions. Studies of the peoples of the forests and the savannahs prompted anthropologists to follow a different line of investigation – but one that still involved language and the sovereign power that it wielded in the earliest days of the human race. This was the power of naming, of creating sounds and giving them meaning. For Tylor too, the primordial state of humanity to which native peoples alive in his own day continued to testify made it possible to understand why, in the beginning, all languages are governed by the same 'intellectual art'.

The coincidence of language and myth is a sign of the earliest times for human beings, when a real life was attributed to nature as a whole and when language exerted a full and total tyranny over the human mind. In conditions such as these, mythology is everywhere, impregnating grammar, invading syntax, proliferating in metaphors. But mythology only possesses that force for a while, at the very beginning of the development of the human mind. It is a time of childhood that will pass away as the human mind evolves and necessarily reaches maturity: next comes the time of reason and philosophy. Mythology reveals the human mind in its primordial state. It falls to anthropologists to observe it on the African continent, in the Americas, wherever they can encounter 'savage' peoples – that is to say representatives of the human race who are still 'at the stage of creating myths'.

The basic assumption is that in the beginning the human mind 'mythologizes' spontaneously. Myth and language evolve contemporaneously, testifying to a first stage of thought that has an autonomy of its own and that needs to be observed and analysed. Tylor postulated the existence of thought of a mythical kind, with characteristics sufficiently specific to enable historians and anthropologists alike to recognize it immediately wherever it appears, either directly or indirectly. Myth is *a natural and regular product of the human mind reacting to particular circumstances* and in such circumstances, Tylor declares, the human mind is bound to mythologize. That proposition comes quite close to what Claude Lévi-Strauss was to say, in the 1960s, about savage thought. But there is one major difference. For Tylor, myth, that spontaneous cultural product of the human mind, is a sign of childishness and weakness. For him, the intellectual art that mythology represents is a 'philosophy of the nursery'. For Lévi-Strauss, in contrast, the savage thought that is manifested freely in a body of myth is complex and involves a wealth of intellectual operations. It is true that, in Greece, for example, it was to 'desist' and give way to philosophy, the philosophical thought that emerged there 'as the necessary forerunner to scientific reflection' (a subject to which we shall be returning). But from Tylor onwards, right down to the present day, mythology became an essential element in the functioning of the human mind.

Mythical thought among philosophers and sociologists

Anthropologists are not usually prone to read philosophers, and vice versa. Nevertheless, it was a German philosopher, Schelling, who in 1856 published the fundamental work on mythology. In his *Introduction to the Philosophy of Mythology*, Schelling's speculative idealism showed that a basic inclination of the human mind is manifested in mythology. It involves a kind of process that is necessary to consciousness and has nothing to do with inventiveness. Schelling sets out to reconcile the monotheism of reason and the polytheism of the imagination within a rational mythology. He constructs a theogony of the Absolute, thereby alerting Ernst Cassirer and Marcel Mauss to the fact that the only way to interpret myth correctly is to adopt a 'tautegorical' method. In other words, the meaning of myth lies in what it recounts, not elsewhere. In Germany, in the wake of Cassirer's neo-Kantian scholarship, Walter F. Otto cultivated the values of epiphany and of the revelation of the sacred, which emerged as specific features of myth and are still considered to be so today. Greece, par excellence, produced a body of myth that testifies to what Otto, among others, calls 'original experience *made manifest*' – experience that, as he sees it, is also what makes rational thought possible.

Alongside the philosophical and spiritual path opened up by Schelling, we should be aware of a parallel track, which was to be particularly favoured by philosophy and historicism. Before becoming a rut, this was the route that the poet-historian Karl

Otfried Müller (1797–1840) had opened up in the early nineteenth century. In his view mythology is certainly a form of thought marked by the naivety and simplicity of the earliest times, but it takes shape slowly, reflecting the impact of events and circumstances. Understanding this essential product of the human mind involves rediscovering an original landscape and fathoming the realities that led human intelligence to articulate relations in the form of actions that, more often than not, revolve around a proper name, in an original story. For this traveller, both a Romantic and a historian, the land of myths was a forgotten world, which could be recalled by discovering the landscape that alone could authenticate the story produced long ago by that particular locality. K. O. Müller thus introduced a way of analysing mythology that was to continue for a long time to fascinate historians and philologists dealing with antiquity. It consisted in stripping away from myths the concretions that, in the course of time, had rendered them unrecognizable, and then – courtesy of Pausanias or some other ancient traveller who, for his part, had truly seen and heard – getting through to some home-grown stories and replacing these in their historical and geographical context.

On the subject of mythical consciousness and mythical thought, Durkheim's sociology was to rival the philosophy of Cassirer, while at the same time bestowing upon it the strength of its own convictions. In the first place, Durkheim, as early as 1899, in the first issue of *L'Année sociologique*, set out one of the major theses of *Les Formes élémentaires de la pensée religieuse*: mythology – or religion, for Durkheim made no distinction between them – 'contains within it, right from the start but in a confused state, all the elements which, as they separated out and became defined, interacting in a thousand ways, engendered the divers forms of the collective life'. Then, eleven years later, in 1910, Durkheim repeated his definition of the nature of religion and mythology: this is the most important of all kinds of thought and encompasses everything. It is both itself and more than itself. Mythical thought is no longer seen as a stage in thought, or as a particular phase in the consciousness of the mind. It possesses an astonishing power to engender the fundamental concepts of knowledge and the principal forms of culture.

Durkheim's treatment of this subject was somewhat summary compared to the philosophical approach of Cassirer, who devoted to mythical thought one whole volume of his trilogy, *The Philosophy of Symbolic Forms*. In his analysis *Mythical Thought*, published in 1924, the German philosopher postulated that mythical consciousness defines an autonomous order of knowing and represents a particular mode of human intellectual development. Mythical thought is neither infantile nor feeble. It is an original form adopted by the mind. It is a thought of 'concrescence', the temporal and spatial intuitions of which are concrete and qualitative. Mythical thought, ruled by intuition, is fascinated by the universe that is immediately present and can be apprehended through the senses. Captivated by the contents of intuition, it knows nothing of representation and remains alien to conceptual action. The self engaged in mythical thought, assailed by the desire or fear prompted by every fleeting impression, speaks only haltingly of differences. It distinguishes and separates things, but without ever really pulling free from original, undifferentiated intuition. Here too, myth and language are seemingly inseparable: they constitute two modalities of one and the same impulse towards symbolic expression. Myth is language, but also religion: mythology encompasses the original qualities of both speaking and believing. In the belief that provides the basis for the unity of its experience, mythology is religious thought, or at least potential religion. In mythical experience, religion is already totally present. Mythology, concomitant in language and religion, finds itself assigned a central function in theory regarding the human mind. It constitutes the native soil of all symbolic forms. Right from the start it linked practical consciousness, theoretical consciousness, and the modes of knowledge, art, law and morality, including fundamental models of community and of the state. Virtually all forms of culture are rooted in mythical thought: 'They are all as it were clothed and enveloped by some figure produced by myth.'

Myth, ritual and society

Neither Durkheim nor Cassirer embarked on an interpretation of myths based on their reflections on 'mythical thought'. But others, without the same theoretical ambitions, did devote themselves to interpretation. In 1890 James George Frazer began to publish what became the twelve volumes of *The Golden Bough*. It constitutes an immensely wide-ranging interpretation of myths from all over the world, and allots a prime place to mythical tales drawn from the Greek and Latin authors, which are then compared to those of primitive peoples. Frazer certainly notes all the similarities, paying scant attention to the differences, but his enquiry proceeds along two different paths of investigation. On the one hand, he concentrates on ritual: it was the gestures and practices of ritual that lastingly fashioned cultures, the social subconscious, and the memories that underlie all the major festivals of the human race. On the other hand, he pursues the power and models of transmission, especially the relations between symbolism and power. Frazer sets out to show that human societies develop in three stages: first magic, then religion, then science. He does not regard mythology as the particular province of a type of thought with an autonomy of its own.

For sociological historians in France, such as Marcel Granet and Louis Gernet, the analysis of myths in China and in Greece seemed to open up a splendid approach to different forms of thought. Both subscribed to the hypothesis, theorized by Antoine Meillet and Emile Benveniste, that language conveys concepts and thereby itself imparts form to institutions. Vocabulary is not so much a lexicon as a conceptual system; it is organized around categories that refer to institutions – that is to say, to the guiding schemata that are present in techniques, modes of life and the procedures of speech and thought. Marcel Granet and Louis Gernet, while regarding 'institutions' as a kind of historical subconscious, concentrate upon the mode of thought that they call now mythical, now mythico-legendary or mythico-religious. In the civilizations of both China and Greece, mythical thought, the depository of the fundamental frameworks of ancient thought, can be apprehended only through remains, fragments, vestiges: the vestiges and remains of a unitary and all-encompassing thought that finds expression only in certain myths, not in the whole mythical corpus that is accessible, at least in Greece, in 'mythographic' forms.

Like the China of the warring states period, archaic Greece reveals itself as one of those places in which the enquiries of sociological historians can uncover mythical data in which 'much of the social subconscious' is deposited. The investigations of Louis Gernet, so innovative in the Hellenist studies of the first half of the twentieth century, revealed mythical data associated with the traditions of both ancient royal houses and peasant phratries. In the course of about thirty years, Gernet's 'attentive reading' centred upon traditions of sovereignty, along with images of gift-giving, challenges, treasures, tests and sacrifices, and also upon a whole rural fund of beliefs and practices amid which people cele-brated, feasted, entered into marriage alliances, and confronted one another in competitions. In those particular fragments at least, Greek mythology seems to offer the sociologist access to a real society whose image is reflected clearly in myth, while at the same time it presents the historian of 'prehistoric patterns of behaviour' with a whole store of religious and legal notions that were to be deployed within the space of the future city.

On the place of the Greeks and abstraction

Through their enquiries and thanks to the very nature of their field, Greek scholars interested in 'archaeology' have revealed that the investigations into mythology and mythical thought carried out by Tylor, Durkheim and Cassirer all have a common horizon. When Louis Gernet, in his essay 'The Origins of Philosophy', showed how important it is to define what 'mythical concepts, religious practice and the very forms of society contributed to the schemata of the emerging philosophy', he was referring explicitly to the Greek context. It was in archaic Greece, not in Oceania, some African city, or even China, that Western observers noted how myth and mythical thought had come to be overtaken. Greece was the *exceptional* place in which there occurred what Hellenists call, quite simply, 'the transition from mythical thought to positivist abstract thought' or, more snappily, 'from myth to reason'. Since the thought of the eighteenth century BC at least, the Greeks had occupied a strategic position, for they were in command of the frontier between fable and religion, between myth and philosophy. The Greeks represented by Homer and Parmenides command a view over the narrow defile in which myth was overtaken by philosophical thought. They are, indeed, totally identified with both that landscape and its conceptual description. Cassirer, being a philosopher, understood better than others to what extent the data and the formulation of the problem are Greek and are indissolubly linked.

Today, even after the advances made in comparative studies of Greece, China and India, no historical or intellectual configuration seems so forcefully to present the spectacle, almost unchallengeable to *our Western eyes*, of this emergence of philosophy: a new kind of philosophical thought against a background of mythology and mythical traditions. Neither in ancient China nor in Vedic or Brahmanic India does there seem to have existed first such a contiguity, then such a distance, between the major recounted myths and forms of abstract or positivist thought as is to be found in archaic Greece. Based on that account perhaps, divergent interpretations have been produced not only among Greek scholars working on close analyses of forms of rupture and continuity, but also among the sociologists, philosophers and anthropologists motivated by an understanding of how thinking changes. As Durkheim saw it, an 'engendering', in the form of a demystification, took place: thanks to the Greeks – that is, to the philosophers of Greece – mythology gave birth to a universe of concepts. Cassirer, who is more attentive to local configurations of thought, spoke of a 'misunderstanding' of mythic consciousness and emphasized the aspect of overtaking and new understanding: 'a true overtaking of myth must be spurred by an understanding and recognition of it'.

On the overtaking of myth

Overtaking, abstraction, emerging: all these metaphors are applicable in this frontier area. In his *Mythologiques*, Claude Lévi-Strauss describes mythical thought as moving towards abstraction and strong enough to contemplate 'a world of concepts in which relations are freely defined'. By 1966 he had converted that 'being overtaken' into 'a withdrawal'. A frontier was reached and 'mythology *withdrew* in favour of philosophy, which emerged as the precondition for scientific thought'.

For Lévi-Strauss, as for Cassirer, the situation was more complicated than one simply of overtaking or discreetly withdrawing. For
mythology to be understood and its essential elements recognized,
what was needed was the intellectual mastery of the Greeks, above
all the Greek philosophers, who were the first to set about interpreting this 'pre-historical' thought. To Lévi-Strauss, the Greek
paradigm seemed so meaningful that, faced with various readings
of Greek myths that he himself had inspired, he remarked that the
ancient Greeks 'seem to have perceived and thought through their
mythology in terms of a procedure that was to some degree ana-
logous to that followed today by ethnologists attempting to discover the spirit and meaning of the myths of illiterate peoples'. The
primacy of the Greek example was now fully acknowledged: the
culture of the Greeks presented the spectacle of mythical thought
that, reaching beyond itself, acceded to a logic of Forms on the basis
of which Greeks, equipped with concepts, set about thinking
through their mythology and interpreting it.

Now that the Greek paradigm has been recognized, let us return
to those ancients whom the founders of the science of mythology
claimed as their immediate precursors: those 'pious and thoughtful'
men of early Greece, such as Xenophanes of Colophon and Plato.
For it was they and others like them who were the first to 'try to
find explanations for beliefs closely linked to religion yet which
seemed a negation of both religion and morality'. Those were the
terms in which the contemporaries of Max Müller and Tylor spoke
of mythology: stories described as beliefs, which oscillated between
religion and irreligion. Moderns seem to imitate the ancients and to
find in their ways of proceeding the best of reasons for acting as they
did and agreeing to call certain stories myths – stories that, once collected, are referred to as mythology, if not mythical thought itself.

We shall return to this point later, in connection with analytical
procedures, so at this point it suffices to remark that it is perhaps
inevitable to believe, as Lévi-Strauss did at the beginning of his
long and admirable voyage of discovery, that 'throughout the
whole world a myth is perceived as a myth by all its *readers*'. So it
is all the more useful to show the readers, who we all are, the extent
to which, even among the Greeks themselves, the category of
'myth' eluded the kind of simple and positive definition that we

might expect from those who were apparently the first to set about thinking through their own mythology (if that is what we decide to call it).

What the Greeks called 'myth'

As suggested above, the interpretation of the great stories of the Greek tradition began in the sixth century BC, with the earliest philosophers. If we are to reflect upon *interpretation* in its earliest form – in ancient Greece, at least – we must first distinguish it from *exegesis*. Exegesis may be defined as the ongoing commentaries that a culture produces on its symbolism, its behaviour and its practices – everything that constitutes it as a system in action. Exegesis proliferates from within. It is speech that nurtures the tradition to which it belongs. Interpretation, in contrast, begins at the point where an external perspective develops – when, in a society, some people begin to argue about the tradition and criticize it, distancing themselves from the stories of their tribe. The process of looking with an outsider's eye at what is accepted by everyone else may take at least two different forms. In Greece, one form, which was minimal, began with the prose writing of those whom the fifth century came to call *logographers*. For the past century already, they had been arranging, within the new space created by writing, traditional accounts and stories ranging from genealogies to long heroic epics. But in parallel to that discreet and silent distancing procedure produced solely through the operation of writing, a second process was developing, in a form that made a major impact. It found expression through new modes of thought that were inseparable from writing, such as the early philosophy of Xenophanes of Colophon and the conceptualized history of Thucydides: modes of thought that radically called into question a tradition now condemned as unacceptable or no longer credible, for it made no immediate sense and did not seem to have any deeper meaning.

The initial interpretation

In the way that myth was interpreted, a new concept of myth was formed, and the image of mythology, in the Greek sense of *mythologia*, in all its specificity, emerged. In the history of the period between the sixth and the early fourth century, a series of landmarks help to define how the territory assigned to *mythos* was organized. In about 530 Xenophanes, in the name of the fledgling philosophy, forcefully rejected the whole collection of stories about Titans, Giants and Centaurs, including those purveyed by Homer and Hesiod. They constituted a pack of scandalous adventures that set on stage gods or superhuman beings and featured all that was offensive and deplorable in the world of human beings, such as theft, adultery and deceit. Xenophanes rejected all traditional tales of that kind, assigning them a twofold status. In the first place they were forgeries, *plasmata*, or pure fictions; and secondly, they were barbarian stories, tales told by 'others'. But the word *mythos* – which, ever since epic, had been part of Greek vocabulary, speech or language – was not yet mobilized to designate the discourse at which philosophy, barely established yet already scandalized, was pointing the finger and which it was so insistently denouncing. At about the same time, however, a poem by Anacreon of Samos gave the term *mythos* a new meaning. Between 524 and 522, the party of Samian rebels who rose up against the tyranny of Polycrates was known as the party of the *mythietai*. As the ancient grammarians explained, these were factious men, troublemakers or probably, to be more precise, people who spread seditious talk. *Myth* thus meant revolution, *stasis*, the opposite of the *eunomia* advocated by Polycrates. Then, in the course of the fifth century, this semantic development, to which Anacreon's poem happens to testify, took a more precise turn in the vocabulary of Pindar and Herodotus, where the word 'myth', still used quite sparingly, came to designate simply such discourse of 'others' as was illusory, incredible or stupid. In works such as Herodotus's *Histories* and Pindar's *Epinicians*, which seem to accommodate a large number of what we should be tempted to call 'myths', the occurrences of the word *mythos* can be counted on the fingers of one hand: it appears only twice in the nine books of Herodotus's *Histories* (II. 23, 45) and three times in Pindar's *Odes* (*Nemean*, 7.23–24, 8.25–26; *Olympian*, 1.27–59). When Pindar sings the praises of a victor in the Games, he is pronouncing a *logos*; myth only makes its appearance with *parphasis*, the speech of illusion. It is rumour that engenders *mythos*. It flourishes with deceptive accounts, with twisted words that are seductive but violate the truth. Fashioned like one of Daedalus's statues, *mythos* is detectable from its motley of lies. It creates appearances that fake credibility and constitute a shameful betrayal of the manifestation of 'what is'. But myths are always stories told by 'others', by those who have usurped the renown well deserved by Ajax but now credited to Odysseus, or those who spread abroad a scandalous version of the banquet of Tantalus, in which the gods are represented as having feasted greedily upon slices of Pelops's flesh.

Herodotus makes the same distinction. His own accounts are always proper discourse, *logoi*. And when referring to particularly holy traditions, Herodotus always calls them sacred (*hieroi logoi*). The famous 'sacred discourse' that *we* would call 'myths' – particularly as the traditions are often associated with ritual actions and gestures – is never referred to as *mythoi*. As Herodotus sees it, when people try to explain the flooding of the Nile by blaming the immensity of the river Ocean that surrounds the earth, that is a myth, for it is a fiction pure and simple, which excludes any kind of rational argument and can accommodate no empirical observation. And when Greeks claim that Busiris, the king of the Egyptians, tried to sacrifice Heracles, that too is a myth, for it is stupid and absurd: how could the Egyptians, the most pious of all men, even dream of committing such a grave impiety?

To speak of *myth* is a way of evoking scandal and pointing the finger at it. *Mythos* constitutes an extremely convenient word-gesture, the effect of which is to indicate stupidity, fiction or absurdity and, at the same stroke, to condemn it. But as yet *myth* is still something vague, something distant and ill-defined. Not until the very end of the fifth century did it come to designate a more or less autonomous discourse or form of knowledge. At that point, both the stories of the ancient poets and all that the logographers had been writing swung over on to the side of *mythos*. One of the contexts in which this division took place was the history written by Thucydides, for he defined the field of historical knowledge by excluding the fabulous, or *mythodes*, from his conceptual territory and assigning it to a separate domain that took over a quite different way of recounting and recording things.

The choices of Thucydides

The logographers set tribal stories down in writing. Herodotus
aimed to provide the city with a new store of memories.
Thucydides, for his part, set out to construct a model for political
action, an understanding of future possibilities, with the historian
regarded as an ideal political leader. He aimed not to recount what
had happened, but to convey the truth in discourse made up of
arguments so well constructed that, more effectively than any
other means, it indicated how best to behave within the space of
the city, both in the present and in the future. However, a history
of present times, such as *The Peloponnesian War*, is bound to face
problems posed by memory and the oral tradition. Thucydides
does so in what is now known as an *Archaeology*, in which hearsay
stories are criticized. Memory is fallible, for there are holes in it;
besides which, it interprets, selects and reconstructs, and the
more troubled the times, the more marvels proliferate, and the
more everything becomes credible, the more unreliable it is. In
Thucydides' view, all that circulates orally, all that is *akoai*, is fundamentally erroneous on account of the absence of a critical spirit
on the part of people who recount or report what happened
yesterday or in the past, even in their own land where they could
become better informed, and could check out and correct their
stories. Traditional memory is judged guilty of accepting ready-
made ideas and of credulously spreading unverified information
that swells the flood of *fable*. Poets and logographers are included
among the accused in the charges brought against hearsay, for
rumours, ready-made ideas, which in any case fall into the category
of what is incredible, are no longer at all believable when the poets
turn them into stories, endowing the events with splendours that
make them more impressive, and when, in parallel fashion, the
logographers set about combining several ready-made ideas with
the idea of pleasing the ear rather than establishing the truth. With
Thucydides, the distinction becomes cut and dried: on the one
hand, there is tradition, which continues to express itself even in
the public recitations and pronouncements of the late fifth
century; on the other, writing, now sure of itself, which rejects pleasure and marvels, and is aimed at a silent, solitary reader. The

author of *The Peloponnesian War* is convinced that anything passed on by word of mouth inevitably degenerates into fable – that is to say, into all that tends to block the efficacy of discourse conveyed by abstract writing and designed to reinforce action of a political nature.

The mythology of the city in Plato

Alongside Thucydides, and contemporaneously, the overarching thought constituted by the philosophy of Plato proceeded, with even greater rigour, to separate out what Plato and his contemporaries labelled, on the one hand, *mythology* and, on the other, *archaeology*. The radical critique aimed, through the poets and craftsmen of *logoi*, at the entire tradition singled out the mimetic character of *mythology* – that is to say, modes of expression with formulaic, rhythmic and musical aspects that catered for the needs of memorization and oral communication but that, for a philosopher, constituted irrefutable evidence of belonging to the polymorphous world of all that appealed to the lower part of the soul, that separate realm where passions and desires run riot. Not only was the discourse of mythology scandalous – and the *Republic* listed all its obscene, savage, and absurd stories – but it was also dangerous, on account of the misleading effects created by hearsay whenever it eluded surveillance and control.

However – and this constituted the major difference from Thucydides – while it was easy enough, in the ideal city, to ban the ancient beliefs and to get rid of the poets by dint of censoring the traditional stories, the Platonic plan to reform the crisis-stricken city made it necessary to invent and fashion a different, 'new' *mythology* – *a fine, useful lie*, capable of ensuring that all and sundry freely did whatever was right. Plato's *Laws*, in particular, contains an intuitive and spectral analysis of what constitutes a 'tradition': rumour that ranges from malicious gossip repeated by others all the way to discourse inspired by the gods; oracles or eulogies that generate great reputations; genealogies constantly evolving; tales about the foundation of cities in the inhabited world; stories that go as far back as Deucalion and Phoroneus; nursery tales, proverbs and sayings; all the kinds of discourse that get repeated over and over again and everywhere win acceptance. No sooner was it liberated from the ancient beliefs than the city strove to recover the secret unity of tradition. For a society, even when conceived and governed by philosophers, needs the only thing that can hold it together: namely, shared and implicit knowledge, thanks to which – as is stressed in the *Laws* (664a) – a community seems to be of one mind throughout its existence, both in its songs and in its stories.

By the beginning of the fourth century, as a result of the combined action of two types of thought – the one philosophical, the other historical – what had furtively been called 'myth' was wiped out, melting away into a new landscape, now known as *mythology*, where mythographers, already professional figures, were to deploy their writing skills.

It was undoubtedly with good reason that the founders of the science of myths recognized Xenophanes and the thinkers of ancient Greece as the initiators of a distinction that they themselves, scholars of the nineteenth century, were happy to ratify. Plato and Thucydides, long before them, certainly were the first to manifest the scandalized reaction that mobilized Müller and Lang once it became clear that the language of mythology was that of a temporarily demented mind. But there was a downside to that prescience, for neither in the nineteenth nor in the twentieth century did any of the shapers of the new science realize quite how strange this 'mythology' was: this concept that had stemmed from that ancient attempt at classification and that, ever since, has continued to prompt the most diverse of questions.

The practices of myth-analysis

In the 1950s, things being as they are, despite the progress made by Georges Dumézil, within the small circle of practising mythologists no great upheavals could be expected – especially where *our* Greeks were concerned. Fortunately though, between 1958 and 1964, in France and primarily at the Ecole pratique des hautes études (Sciences religieuses), Claude Lévi-Strauss, an Americanist, embarked upon a radically new reading of mythical stories. Some hasty interpreters soon produced a handful of formulas in which they summarized the implicit philosophy. These, swept up in the fashion for structuralism, almost immediately blocked the development of any thought on the actual procedures followed in this very new way of analysing familiar stories. The ignorance and vanity of those who rushed to sport post-structuralist T-shirts created such misunderstanding that today it is more helpful to speak of the practices adopted in the analysis of myths than to become bogged down in arguments over signs, texts and out-of-date semiotics.

Since Herman Usener and Marcel Mauss, mythology, as it is generally understood, has been perceived as an inevitable kind of social thought, but on a subconscious level. For Mauss, mythology could be reduced to a handful of combinations: 'A myth is one stitch in a spider's web.' Lévi-Strauss, for his part, was from the start more interested in the spider and its instinctive understanding of geometry. Mythical thought, the savage mind, mythology believed to be universal consists of a manifold of forms from the oral tradition produced by a particular kind of mind, 'a mind that refuses to accept a partial answer and seeks explanations that incorporate the totality of phenomena'. On the one hand, there is a 'mind' faced by a single problem; on the other, a way of proceeding that involves considering that problem to be homologous to other problems that arise at other levels – cosmological, physical, juridical, social and moral – and accounting for all of them at once. That is one way of defining mythology, which stresses the multiplicity of levels of meaning, but does not pause to consider the diversity of contexts that any analysis must address. However, it by no means excludes another definition that Lévi-Strauss would be happy to endorse. It is a native definition produced by an Amerindian teller of myths: a myth is 'a story of the time when men and animals were not yet distinct'. A time before, a cosmogonic state, a story from before the beginnings, which, however, is not frozen in pre-philosophical discourse.

There are, then, two ways of perceiving mythology and, it would seem, of analysing it: either as a system of representation that always goes beyond the narrative genre devoted to one particular aspect of the mythology, or as a narrative genre, a domain organized by certain modes of narration. The latter model seemed at first to have triumphed with the idea, so quickly accepted and unreservedly appropriated, that 'myth is language' and that a myth must be broken down into mythemes, the distinct units that make up this language, units from which a semiotic analysis of the myths will soon produce a narrative grammar. It seemed to me, as I have said before, that Claude Lévi-Strauss's initial proposition in his *Mythologiques* – namely that 'throughout the whole world, a myth is perceived as a myth by all its readers' – was tenable, provided one avoided the pitfall of a 'narrative genre' and the 'mythemes' of a natural metalanguage.

Relationships, transformations, contexts

Yet, following those experiments in semiotico-linguistics, the first of those two ways of perceiving mythology seems to have won out, thanks to the analytical procedures developed by Lévi-Strauss in works ranging from his *Geste d'Asdiwal* to the last of his *Mythologiques* volumes, and *La Potière jalouse (The Jealous Potter)* and *Histoire de lynx (The Story of Lynx)*. Three concepts may help to define this type of analysis: relations, transformations and contexts. The first hypothesis concerns relationships: terms considered in isolation never convey an intrinsic meaning. Meaning stems from how they are opposed to one another; it depends upon interrelationships. The second proposition is that the analysis of a myth involves studying the transformational relationships among the various versions of the myth and between that myth and others related to it. In other words, neither one single version nor a synthesis of several versions constitutes an adequate subject for study. The third principle is that this type of analysis requires an understanding of the ethnographic context, one that is *independent* of the mythical material itself and that embraces the whole collection of objects, values and institutions that constitute the culture of the society in which the myths chosen by the analyst are recounted. Plants, animals, customs, geographical data, ecological systems, astronomical phenomena, techniques: the interpreter-decipherer of myths needs to acquire knowledge of all these in the manner of a native encyclopaedist. For beneath such a wealth of details – some curious, others unremarkable – the analyst will discover the multiple levels of meaning that make up the thick fabric of the mythical account. The analyst must mobilize all the different registers of the culture in question – its plants, animals, foodstuffs, hunting methods, fishing techniques, astronomical calendars – and must do so in as many societies as seem necessary, judging from a comparison of closely related or contrasting myths. Contrary to the vaguely semiotic perceptions of those who have neither practised it nor understood it, the structural analysis of myths involves not only the myths themselves but also an understanding of the concrete circumstances of the relevant societies and experimentation with their intellectual structures, sometimes in a limited local context, sometimes in a wider one. The analyst needs to work using several levels of meaning; at each level, latent properties may be extracted from the domain under investigation that allow it to be compared to other domains.

Although such analysis combines many elements, it is not necessarily interminable. Like all forms of interpretation, the structural analysis of myths accepts certain constraints and sets itself certain limits – in the first place, those affecting the particular culture in which the myths circulate. The said culture may well, thanks to the richness of its myths and the wide range of their different versions, present a field vast enough to allow the analyst who has selected certain abstract schemata (which another analyst may well leave aside) to reconstruct an organized semantic context and to interweave elements that seem to belong to the same configuration. It is a procedure that certainly enriches the myths rather than diminishes them by reducing them to a small number of skeletal oppositions. And if the analyst chooses to limit the enquiry to the parameters of one particular society, he or she may have reason to hope, by restricting the field of comparison around one constellation of myths together with their distinct versions, to discover more possible differences and distinctions, and thereby to enrich the culture with a new set of qualitatively different relations.

Mythology as a framework and mythology as lore

This type of analysis, which pays attention to the correspondences among several semantic levels and chooses to open up each mythical account to other related traditions and stories, is not content merely to discover the odd conceptual mechanism here or there. It suggests that mythical stories are transformed as they are passed on. The hypothesis of 'the mythical' introduced by Lévi-Strauss perhaps makes it possible to move beyond the idea that mythical thought thinks itself. Let us assume that each story that is told is the work of one individual. No sooner does it emerge from the lips of the first narrator than it enters the oral tradition or, at least, is tested by the mouths and ears of others. To explain how a story becomes 'unforgettable', Lévi-Strauss suggests drawing a distinction between structured levels and possible levels: the former, which rest upon communal foundations, will remain stable; the latter, which depend upon approbation, will manifest an extreme variability, which stems from the personalities of their successive narrators. Put another way, in the process of becoming part of the communal memory, whatever each individual narrator is responsible for – through his way of adding certain details or leaving others out or of expanding certain episodes and omitting others – is different in nature from that which roots the story in the tradition that produces it and that it in turn produces. In the course of oral transmission, as the continuous chain of narrators unfolds, the possible levels clash, are worn away, and progressively separate out from the mass of the discourse what might be called 'the crystalline parts' – that is, the parts that confer a more regular structure or 'a greater symbolic meaning' upon a traditional story. As Lévi-Strauss says in the conclusion to *L'Homme nu* (1971) (*The Naked Man*, 1981), 'The individual works are all potential myths, but it is their collective adoption that, in particular cases, actualizes their *mythism*.'

Once 'the mythical' is recognized as one of the major phenomena of memorability in cultures of the spoken word (rather than call them 'traditions that must remain oral'), 'myth', as a literary genre or a narrative of a particular kind, begins to be set in a category apart. This leads to the discovery of the diversity of the works that preserve memories: proverbs, tales, genealogies, cosmogonies, epics and songs of love or war. Myth comes in many registers, and each society is free to choose particular ones and to theorize about them. In each of those registers variation is at work through repetition, and each is subjected to a similar process of selection. Just as, from this perspective, it would be illusory to suppose that any myth is immediately recognizable as a myth, the mythology of a society does not necessarily immediately coincide with what appears to be its mythology, nor with what the society, left to itself, calls 'mythology'. A structural analyst, in quest of the concrete elements that will make it possible to penetrate the levels of meaning of accounts possibly belonging to very different genres, knows perfectly well that certain proverbs, nursery songs, or episodes in sacrificial ceremonial are, in many cases, essential for a detailed understanding of what has become an exemplary story or for the construction of a conceptual schema that will reveal the interactions of two versions of the same narrative.

Plato, an observer of human beings better known as a philosopher, was well aware of the full range of what must be called 'mythology' in Greece itself, the place where mythology – the whole collection of stories about gods and heroes – had become a particularly Greek category, thanks to the mediation of those soon to be known as 'mythographers', who set about composing collections of those stories, keeping them quite separate from other traditional pronouncements. Given that it was Greece that provided the rest of the world with the category of 'mythology', we should point out that in the home of Plato and Pindar two types of mythology coexisted: mythology as a framework and mythology as lore. Mythology as a framework consists of a system of thought that is revealed, or rather *reconstructed*, by structural analysis – that is to say, the more or less complex, all-encompassing system that extends throughout Greek culture, with all its beliefs, practices and different types of accounts (among which those of Hesiod and Homer are simply better known than the rest). Meanwhile, mythology as knowledge, prepared by 'native theologians', was written partly by the early logographers or historians, partly by the authors of the mythographic works that culminated in the *Library* attributed to Apollodorus that, in about AD 200, was revealing the full cultural richness of mythology in Greek society over a period of seven or eight centuries.

The more these ways of analysing myths are developed, the better we shall come to understand some of the mental mechanisms that underlie cultural competence – that is, the body of representations that any individual, as a member of a society, must possess in order to think and to act. Furthermore, anthropologists studying polytheistic civilizations will discover even more of the secret complexity of the systems of gods and the representations of supernatural powers that are so often built into the architecture of the myths and the great, unforgettable narratives of so very many societies.

3

Transcribing Mythologies:
From Japan and New Caledonia to the Pontiffs of Rome

For us, even today, the Greeks are still the initiators of a development that led from myth towards mythology. Their audacity continues to mark our thinking about the traditional relations between mythology and mythography and the possible connection between myth, writing and forms of historicity. In his later writing, Plato provides useful testimony of the most common meaning of 'tradition': that which is handed on orally, that which comes to us from the ancients. Plato had a word for whatever is transmitted and appears to have been always believable: 'mythology'. In the context of the Greeks themselves, 'mythology' refers us both to those whom he calls 'collectors', that is to say Hesiod and Homer, and also to those whom he describes as 'enquiring', men of leisure who set themselves to seek out ancient traditions. In Greece, the transcription of stories and traditions was progressively to spread, developing along a whole set of ramified paths.

Happily, the question of writing and mythology, although also of a local nature, extends beyond the boundaries of the homeland of our Greeks. Not so long ago, I made the deliberately provocative statement, 'Mythology is something that is written down'.[1]

When I read that a myth is perceived as a myth by *every reader throughout the entire world*,[2] I remarked that 'throughout the entire world' seemed to raise difficulties. Basically, the transcription of mythologies raises the same problems but they come over with greater force if, when we call attention to various societies perceived, in some cases, from afar and in others, perhaps, from closer to, we ask ourselves the following question: what happens when mythology, mythological tradition, is captured in writing and is, either forcefully, firmly or even gently, embedded in writing? What happens when it is placed wholly or partially in the hands of scribes or other writers or – worse still – when in its written form it is shut away in some mausoleum? What happens when certain more or less indigenous people set about reworking the stories of the past, the great myths and traditional discourse, wielding their reed-pens, styluses and scalpels, all the tools dreamed up by the tribe of writers?

To inject a spirit that would lift such a question out of those pedestrian formulations, I needed the right opportunity and the luck to stumble upon other individuals with similar preoccupations. Fortunately, I read and met contemporary anthropologists who were likewise asking themselves, what is a tradition? How is it formed and transmitted? What happens when traditions are written down? What effects does that writing produce even in the innermost layers of the long histories of so many diverse societies living oceans apart?

In the company of those anthropologists, comparativism seemed a promising approach, and not one of us was afraid to leave their native homeland behind and set sail for expanding horizons that offered cultural experiences and variations on a scale to match the map that has been growing richer by both day and night ever since the sixteenth century, when explorers were setting out from all our respective bases.[3]

From Japan to the land of the Kanaka

I was lucky enough to chance upon a scene in the Japanese style when François Macé,[4] with supporting textual evidence at the ready, told me how, in the space of a few years, the central power, that of the first imperial household, having acquired full authority, ordered that 'the facts of the past', cosmogonic traditions, stories about the gods and the history of the first sovereigns of Japan, should all be recorded in writing. For many years, distinguished Hellenists have been wrestling with the problem of Greek poets who dictated their work and those who did not, either shunning writing or trying to conceal its presence. Now, all of a sudden (unless, that is, they had perchance glimpsed what was coming), they were confronted with the spectacle of writing taking over and setting a body of material in order in a manner never seen on their own terrain but that presented certain comparable elements, even if these interacted in different ways.

Now for a shift of scene. A reader of ethnological literature very quickly learns that the telling of great stories, whether exotic or not, is often ruled by strict practices: the stories have to be told, recited or sung in specially selected places and within suitable contexts. Furthermore, the narrative form resists written notation. It is even claimed that sometimes the storytellers themselves no longer recognize their own stories and, once these are fixed in written words, they reject them. The diligent administrators of the past, whose duty it was to write them down, were clearly scandalized by this.

Around the 1930s in New Caledonia, ethnologists introduced, along with their own modern customs, the practice of writing, even of writing about oneself. Writing had long been practised in Western cultures and now, in Kanaka territories inhabited by Protestant priests, was activated by ethnologists working there. Attracted or converted by these pale-skinned visitors, the Melanesians adopted the habit of noting down their own stories and histories. They set about composing 'mythology notebooks' and in the process translated their myths from performances in local contexts to general readability. These Melanesian intellectuals, who were encouraged by their Protestant culture to look beyond their local horizons, now began to get to know one another as they worked together with words. Gradually, within the space of a few decades, they put together a preliminary version of a general mythology, focusing it on the people known as the 'Kanaka'. During the 1970s, these intellectual mythographers, who were deeply committed to the independence movement, undertook to forge the identity of the Kanaka people, united in their struggle for decolonization. Under the charismatic influence of Jean-Marie Tjibaou, these Melanesian contemporaries picked out certain major traditional themes and created a completely new figure: the autochthonous Kanaké, the original man and primordial representative of all the Kanaka.[5] Before our very eyes, a history was invented, partly myth, partly memories, and very similar to the history that a fourteenth-century land called France had created for itself, thanks to the efforts of monks skilled in calligraphy and the court of one particular lesser royal figure.[6]

Japan and Melanesia constituted two new discoveries that both seemed to show glimpses of configurations offering ways both similar and different of fixing mythology, historicizing traditions and creating pasts that could measure up to their very different present situations. Here were two scenes that suddenly 'disrupted' the original and commonsensical 'Greek' configuration with its first example of a historiography that seemed to flow eternally from the inborn rationality of our Greeks.

In the case of Japan, one senses a real breakthrough: in the space of ten to fifteen years, there were ruptures, changes and new beginnings. A series of decisions made by the central power confirmed its authority: the establishment of a fixed capital, written laws (for whom? one wonders), censuses, land registers and calendars. Two separate committees were created to set Japanese traditions down in writing. Japan thus took shape by setting up an internal opposition: the *Kojiki*, an 'account of primordial times', confirmed the determination of the Japanese to be autochthonous; meanwhile, the *Nihonshoki* (the Annals of Japan) borrowed the techniques of Chinese historiography, and now developed in two forms: on the one hand, Japanese tradition was historicized; on the other, care was taken to cite all variants, in particular of stories about origins. And, as François Macé has pointed out, all this was done as a matter of urgency. The direct beneficiaries of these deliberate policies were the notion of autochthony and the power of the imperial house. However, the mythology written down in the *Kojiki*, for its part, was set to rest in the coffers of the imperial household. Not until the eighteenth century did it re-emerge, as part of an effort to counter Chinese domination. But why was there no sign of a Japanese historiography that might have taken on the interpretation of this tradition set down in writing and thereby have found a way of reflecting upon its 'historicity'?

The practice of writing certainly became established. But there are differences, for in this case the written documents were the responsibility of the central, authoritarian and sovereign power. The notion of a historiographer was too Chinese to have any immediate Japanese future. The fact was that the Japanese way of bringing to life the time of origins in the imperial lineage was not particularly favourable to the creation of an intellectual climate open to autonomous historical knowledge. The proximity of China and the power of Chinese culture seem to have played a crucial part in both this first leap forward by Japan and also its subsequent retreat into isolation. What role did Confucianism play later, perhaps too late, in the history of Japan? What has been the place of historicity (and what kind of historicity?) in Japan's very recent modernity? Another strange aspect revealed by this voyage to Japan is that a great cosmogonical and mythological tradition, once set down in writing, seems to have ground to a halt and unravelled. François Macé tells us that the *Kojiki* was compiled by an official of middling rank who set down in writing what was 'recited' or 'read' to him by a figure 'who had no court rank at all'. In Japan, the tradition of stories seems to have been abruptly broken off.

The God of Israel and his historicity

Let us continue this exercise of experimental comparativism by moving to Israel. In the seventh century BC this was a small kingdom with a level of literacy that was very modest compared to the extremely rich Sumero-Akkadian culture, with its vast libraries, such as that of Assurbanipal. In the eyes of the Babylonians, the Greeks of that time must likewise have seemed illiterate peasants, no better than the barely urbanized nomads of the kingdom of Juda. With Israel, or rather with the Judaism of the double Torah, we enter the passionate field of Revelation. Perhaps a word of explanation would be helpful at this point: this Judaism of the double Torah, the most important strand of Judaism, took shape in the course of the first six centuries of the Christian era.[7] We are told that the Revelation was expressed in three forms: 1. A book, the written Torah that God made known to Moses on Mount Sinai; 2. The oral Torah, transmitted by word of mouth, then progressively set down in writing in the Mishnah, beginning in the

third century AD; 3. The third conveyor of the Revelation was the
sage, or *rabbi*, who still, here and there, embodies the paradigm of
Moses. This Judaism was known as rabbinical or Talmudic, for the
Talmud of Babylon constituted its ultimate authority. Its distinguishing feature was that it laid prime importance upon the *mem-
orized* Torah. Orality and memory maintained their positions in the
face of the competition of the written word.

And what forms do history, historicity and historiography take
in ancient Israel and the Jewish culture? That question has been
tackled by the historian Yosef Yerushalmi in a little book entitled
*Zakhor. Histoire juive et mémoire juive (Zakhor. Jewish History and
Jewish Memory)*.[8] Yerushalmi expresses his surprise upon noting
the absence of the *historian*, as a specific type of man, in the biblical and rabbinical tradition, both in ancient Israel and in the entire
history of Judaism. It is a paradoxical absence, for all our scholarly
experts believe that it was the Jews who, before Christianity,
'invented the meaning of history'. The biblical tradition is full of
what are now called 'historical accounts'; it abounds in royal
chronicles, concrete information and 'historical' figures. As
Yerushalmi points out, the God of Israel is the Lord of *History*. You
might even think he was the best historian in the world, to judge
by his constant appeals always to remember, never to forget the
Covenant, always to treasure the memory of what has happened
to Israel . . . and to no other people: the Revelation offered to
Moses, the will and interventions of the one true God, and the
meaning that the Revelation has definitively imposed upon the
history of his people. Judaism both ancient and modern thus offers
a fine future to memory but no prospects at all to historians, at least
not to the modest kind of scribbler that we like to recognize among
our Greeks and hence to what are accepted to be the origins of
Western culture.

Let us leave Israel and its kingdom for a moment. What was hap-
pening in Greece? Around the twelfth century BC, the ideographic
system of the Mycenaean palaces fell into disuse, along with its
class of scribes. But around the eighth century these people
relearned how to write, when they borrowed and took over an
alphabetic system, transposed, with a few improvements, from the
western Semitic domain: this was the Phoenician alphabet. The

Greeks knew that writing was a recent human invention by close neighbours or possibly by yesterday's Greeks, people a cut above the rest when it came to cleverness. So they allowed neither divination nor manifestations of the gods to obliterate the tradition of writing. Writing was there for the taking and not to be rejected. However, the Greeks had no professional writers, no scribes in the eastern manner, no authoritarian apparatus to exploit writing.[9] On the contrary, their small, dispersed cities made no attempt to appropriate writing but did proceed, here and there, more or less simultaneously, to put it to an altogether new use. This alphabet that was easy to use and to learn made it possible to set down in writing the rules and laws that a community evolved for itself as it opened up a space that was entirely devoted to the discussion of common affairs. However, this *political* use of writing did not exclude other uses that any individual was free to choose. Astronomers and geometricians could seize upon writing just as could sages, philosophers, and all those who, if they enjoyed the requisite leisure, decided to use it to record tradition or, for example, to explain in writing what seemed to them believable among so many unlikely stories. Contrary to rumour among ill-informed philosophers, writing was doing fine in Greece, even in Plato's hands.[10] Each and every member of a political community was obliged to take part in common affairs; but for the rest, he was free to be a philosopher, a geometrician, a poet, or even a historian if his intention was to investigate the recent past, the exploits of men of former times or some sanctuary dedicated to a particular hero, deep in the countryside.[11]

Unlike the Book of Revelation, a Greek city left those who wished to 'do history' a free field in which to operate. In fact it strongly encouraged would-be historians. Why? It is at this point that a comparison between the Greek cities and the Judaic and biblical culture illuminates what it is that makes it possible to research actively into an immediate recent past that is perceived as being separate and distinct from any account of origins.[12] It would seem that thinking about beginnings and providing them with the solidity of an initial event brought about through the will of a human, non-supernatural agent was an entirely alien concept in the world of ancient Israel. This was a society committed to a revealed Book, which counted solely upon one exclusive god and reduced the entire history of Israel to the model of a Covenant between God and his chosen people, bound together by its promises and their obsessive memory of that Covenant. In such circumstances, what meaning could this society ascribe to the idea of an act of 'radical inauguration', a founding accomplished solely through human actions? To be more precise, what could the meaning of 'founding' possibly be in a culture based on *Genesis*, placed under the sign of a divine power that claimed a monopoly over creative power and cultivated 'transcendence'?

Primordial and cosmogonic preoccupations appear to constitute serious obstacles to discourse and thought centred on foundation, and to questioning relating to beginnings. Perhaps an excess of cosmogony rules out thought about human action of an inaugurating nature and with a potential of autonomy, firmly separated from origins and their necessary self-containment. Right down to the end of the second millennium, the whole of the Near East was engaged in writing discourse about origins, tracing the genealogy of the gods, naming the powers who engendered everything, and setting out the hierarchies that organized the world. The creator-gods of Sumer and Babylon fashioned kings in their own image. It was the gods who founded and ruled over the earliest towns and temples. When a Mesopotamian king created a town or sanctuary, he was content simply to repeat the initial gesture of a god up there in the heavens planning a temple or a town. The act of founding was inaccessible to human beings. When, probably at the time of the end of the Exile, the God of Israel proclaimed his transcendence, his quality as a creator was enhanced. Yahweh, the one and only God, now tended to be seen as responsible for the way the world went on in the here and now. It was only later, in Christian thought and through Philo of Alexandria, that he became the creator *ex nihilo*, but already in the Bible he had made it clear that he controlled the whole of humanity. In particular, the Creator had to be the sole founder. From the time of Genesis on, the human and mortal inventors who would establish towns and discover metallurgy and musical instruments would belong to the lineage of Cain, all of them descendants of a murderer.[13] To wish to begin something was to presume to compete with God, to harbour the mad and impious idea of replacing the absolute beginning of creation by a human beginning.

In Greece, however, the gods did not create the world. Although continually present in it, the divine powers were set at a distance from a whole group of activities in which the human race held the initiative. One of the newest of those activities of mortal human beings was beginning, inaugurating, being both the founders and the creators of a political community, which also involved what we, using a term adapted from Latin, call establishing a 'colony'. In reality, though, this was a new city, and dozens or even hundreds of them were soon founded and created by the Greeks, in southern Italy, along the shores of the Black Sea, and along the Ionian coast.

Comparing regimes of historicity

Experimental comparativism was the expression we used as we moved from Japan to New Caledonia and from ancient Israel to archaic Greece, still reserving the possibility of comparing the Rome of the ancient pontiffs with the Bugis-Makassar principalities of the Indonesian world.[14] This comparative enquiry sets out neither to propose a typology nor to compile an inventory of morphologies, but rather to devote itself to an enterprise of construction and experimentation. Tradition, writing and historicity are the three terms that seem to organize our initial enquiry into the possible effects that a regime of historicity sustains from the setting of a tradition or part of a tradition down in writing. Each of those terms is complicated and so by nature problematical, which suggests that we should concentrate on investigating and analysing the most immediate 'approaches' that they seem to open up. A number of remarkable configurations – the Greeks in the basement, Japan with its two modes of historicity on the horizon, Israel with its sense of a history but no historiographers, and so on – are available and to be found in anthropological and historical libraries, either already mobilized or mobilizable. Now that we have adopted the variability of cultures as the object of our study, whether we pursue this at one particular level or take an oblique or angled approach, might not these treasures be brought together in one single, vast library?

These remarkable configurations can be progressively compared, revealing their differences and the particular internal mechanisms that govern them against a background of similarities, as the analyst who chooses to compare them works ceaselessly to construct them and submit them to experimentation. He or she starts from the hypothesis that certain terms are related, that microconfigurations tend to reveal variables, that the form and number of those variables may be defined in an experimental fashion by taking into consideration various cultural manifolds that are available across both time and space. In this particular enquiry of ours, we have concentrated, increasingly explicitly, upon configurations of rupture, of radical transformation, and of beginnings from scratch. This method seems to help us to detect more clearly the effects produced by the introduction of a new technique, the modification of an essential element, or the emergence of a new factor as the result of sudden change. We can also hope to see how more or less close societies behave in or react to situations of rupture or violent beginnings. In this way, we hope to be able to distinguish between, on the one hand, accidental breaks, sudden ruptures and unconscious changes and, on the other, deliberate innovations and willed shifts in the course of a tradition, whether the tradition in question is being criticized, set at a distance or redefined and rethought as part of a decision to alter the course of things.

However ambiguous the word tradition may be,[15] there is no more convenient way to describe the oral transmission from one generation to another of culture and the learning intimately linked with particular practices. When ethnologists used to speak of 'traditional societies', their intention was not so much to oppose them to others 'without traditions', but rather to emphasize the role played by word of mouth in the production and transmission of all the elements of a culture, whether modest or dazzling. In the shared store of memories of a group that is a 'traditional society' (in the sense of the expression explained above), there may of course be great variations in the objects chosen, the absence or presence of 'memory guardians', the modes used for fixing memories (graphic signs, 'ritual texts', collections of stories). In certain societies, such as Japan, the Bugis-Makassar principalities and New Caledonia, the adoption of writing, even when writing takes over

Plate 1 Mount Olympus, dwelling-place of the Olympian gods. Photo by Frédéric Boissonas. © Archives Boissonas

Plate 2 Epidaurus, the theatre and meeting place, dating from the fourth century BC, attributed to the architect Polycleitus the Younger. © René Burri/Magnum Photos

Plate 3 Segesta. The temple itself. Late fifth century BC.
© akg images/Gérard Degeorge

Plate 4 Paestum-Posidonia: abode of Athene. Late sixth-century BC.
© Ferdinando Scianna/ Magnum Photos

Plate 5   Dionysus holding the large drinking vessel, greeting two Maenads who offer him the catch from their hunt over mountain and valley. The Amasis Painter, *c.* 540 BC. Paris, Bibliothèque Nationale, Cabinet des Médailles. © Bridgeman Giraudon

Plate 6 Apollo of Veii pictured as a carnivorous god, *c.* 520–500 BC. Museo di Villa Giulia, Rome. © MP/Leemage

Plate 7 The Trojan Horse in action. Relief Pythos from Mykonos,
c. 670 BC. Mykonos Museum. © akg images

Plate 8 Hoplites in battle, in phalanx formation. Chigi Olpé Corinthian vase,
c. 630 BC. Museo di Villa Giulia, Rome. © akg images/Nimatallah

Plate 9 Agon, or contest of skill, for the funeral of Patroclus. Painting by Sophilus on an urn, c. 580–570 BC. Athens, National Museum © G. Dagli Orti, Paris

Plate 10 (top left) Radiant smile of the Peplos Kore, a young girl or maiden, *c.* 530 BC. Museum of the Acropolis. © akg images/John Hios

Plate 11 (bottom left) Entranced Maenad. Work of Scopas, *c.* 340 BC. Roman copy. Dresden, Staatliche Kunstsammlungen 133. © akg images/Erich Lessing

Plate 12 (bottom right) Hera of Samos, upright in her temple, *c.* 560 BC. Today exiled to the Louvre. © akg images/Erich Lessing

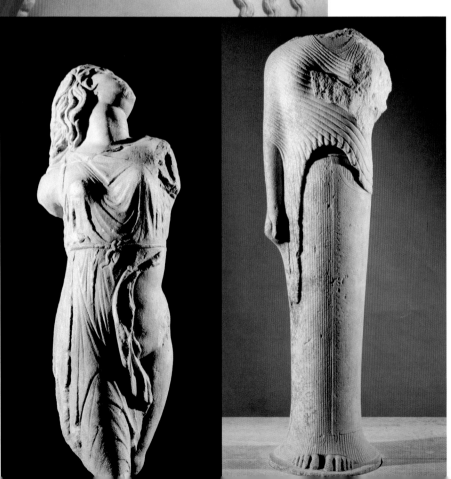

from other ways of fixing tradition, may produce a more or less profound transformation in much of the oral tradition (epics, accounts of origins, founding stories, and so on).

Clearly, the shift to writing may take many diverse forms. Certain cultures as rich as that of China do not seem to have collected great stores of stories at the beginning of their history, nor did ancient Rome or the early Arab culture. The first samples of Chinese writing that constitute an essential part of the ancient tradition served to note down information relating to sacrifices and to interpret the sacrifices in accordance with a divinatory system. The same applies to the Near Eastern civilizations that depended on the activities of scribes to record a body of traditional knowledge. The scribes of Sumer functioned as 'guardians of memory', while rudimentary cultures such as the ancient Israel of the start of the first millennium BC had neither schools of scribes nor any cultural administrative authorities until the eighth century, the date that marks the end of the small kingdom of Juda.

Where writing is concerned, we need to know how it comes to be adopted. Who adopted it, and why? What was its status? The potentialities of writing were fewer in civilizations with values that all conspired to deprecate written documents, such as Vedic India. The same can be said of cultures colonized by the civilization of the New Testament a century and a half ago, which discovered writing through missionaries' translations of the revealed Book. A third example of a similar situation is provided by a world so obsessed with exploring signs detected in the heavens or on the earth that it delegated to a body of technicians the task of establishing the laws that governed such signs, giving them limitless time to do so and placing at their disposal a 'House of Tablets' to work in. This was the body of men who held the highest posts in a kingdom such as Mesopotamia. We must remember that recourse to writing does not necessarily imply that it is recognized to belong to an autonomous domain, nor that there exists any will or power to deploy a 'technology' which, in certain circumstances, would sanction a new intellectual regime. Conversely though, we must not forget that if writing – for example, the writing of the early Greek cities – organizes the public domain and structures the crucial field of politics, its effects on a tradition that turns into 'mythography' will not be the same as in a case where the fixing of memories by graphic or glyphic means is restricted to a closed, if not secret, circle which quietly and deliberately uses writing for its own ends, as among the Cuna people studied by Carlo Severi in the course of a series of expeditions promoted by Sweden.[16]

The reception of a tradition

It is with good reason that ethnologists are beginning to wonder whether it is not the case that they should be paying more attention to the manner in which traditional societies 'receive' their traditions and even, in some cases, regard what is most memorable with a critical eye. Closer attention to the effects of a tradition upon its society would make it possible to produce a more subtle assessment of the impact of a deliberate or radical written version of its memories. Right at the end of the sixth century BC, a Milesian called Hecataeus decided to take the tales of the Greeks, the stories of his tribe, and 'set them down in writing'. He discovered them to be 'multiple', laughed at them and determined to write them down 'as they seemed true to him'.[17] A little later, Herodotus described Hecataeus as a 'maker of stories' (*logopoios*) and eventually other such 'makers of stories', in Japan, New Caledonia, the Southern Celebes and so on, also set to writing. They produced notebooks of 'Kanaka' mythology, 'stories of ancient times' noted down in the court of the first Japanese emperor, and vast epics such as *The Galigo* in the sixteenth-century land of the Bugis-Makassar people.

Whatever its effects, setting a tradition down in writing can, in the immediate or long term, transform a culture founded on orality, memory and whatever is memorable. The written epic of the Indonesians did not affect the authority of speech nor that of the 'language of the gods', but it did progress in parallel towards a double historiography that was at the same time inventing itself in a new political space, complete with 'archivists' and scribes. Meanwhile, in his little Ionian city under threat from the Persians, the logographer Hecataeus, an ordinary citizen, collated the narrative traditions of the Greeks and submitted them to a critique intended for the attention of a handful of other leisured producers of prose like himself.

Whether writing simply arrives or is sought out, it provides a particularly good starting point for thought on the subject of historicity and its modalities in the transition between tradition and historiographical knowledge. Let us suppose that historiography takes off when writing becomes a possibility over and above other procedures for fixing orality and also when a strict or strong separation between the past and the present becomes established. Memories and oral cultures always give way in the face of representations of a time before, with successive stages and temporal reference points. But it would seem that we do not know of many societies with oral cultures that unconsciously turn towards knowledge of the past per se, as to something distinct, cut off from the present. Great 'mythological' traditions may cultivate periodizations and incline towards a marked historicization; but they do not switch spontaneously to historiographical knowledge in the sense understood by the philosophical thought of the Western world that is so confident of its comprehensiveness. Setting about 'constituting' a past is not a self-evident move.

A comparative analysis of regimes of historicity[18] does pay attention to implicit ways of speaking about time and thinking about it and of bringing the past into play and setting it on stage. But it is in contexts of rupture and radical change that it finds a terrain that is eminently favourable for an analysis of practices and ways of thinking about beginnings, foundations and creations that relate to ways of separating the time of the gods from the time of mortals, and the time of the past from that of the present and that of the future. Let us now return to Japan, with its two ways of recording tradition in writing at a time when a centralized power was being established. Japan, which was keen to establish the legitimacy of its imperial family, experimented with two concomitant and parallel ways of proceeding. On the one hand, the *Annals*, with an eye on the present in Japan, recorded dated events set out along a straight temporal line projected from the origin of the world onwards (although, admittedly, the dates involved were selected for their potential to enrich the meaning of the recorded event). Those 'origins' – which included an account of the primordial times of the gods and the very first sovereigns – constituted the major section of the data for the second way of proceeding, that of the *Kojiki*. But the *Nihonshoki* or *Annals of Japan* interpreted that same data altogether differently from the manner chosen by the equally official and deliberate editors of 'stories of ancient times'. Although the *Nihonshoki* collected together all the available traditions on origins, it never mentioned the tradition recorded in the *Kojiki*. The *Annals* presented themselves as an *open* book, a chronicle to be used, whereas the *Kojiki*, which referred back to the work of memorization and recitation of the ancient stories, presented itself as a *closed* book. The *Kojiki* would never be continued. It eschewed dates and avoided allusions to Buddhism and all that the latter brought with it in the way of contemporary history and historicity; it mythologized both the history of the earliest humans and the beginnings of more recent history.

The two traditions' ways of thinking about the foundation of the first capital and the imperial sanctuary of Ise were quite different, as were the ways in which they spoke of, stressed or simply indicated the separate roles of gods and men, and of the times of beginnings and contemporary times. A decision was taken to position the gods well away from the imperial palace and establish them at Ise, in a sanctuary that the emperor would never visit. It was a decision that strengthened the determination to inaugurate a most distinctive history, one that would both adopt the Chinese model of recording 'significant facts' that it would be good to remember, but that would also inhabit a space dominated by an uninterrupted imperial lineage that was not inclined to favour stray Japanese impulses when it came to historicity, new perceptions of time, and reflections on the nature of the past whether recent, distant or extremely distant, that is to say the past of 'the very start of the beginning'.

Pontiffs of the Annals

In the archaic Rome of the kings, had there ever been someone, perhaps even someone without court rank, who recited to one or more scribes an equivalent of the *Kojiki*, all in one go? Where are the great myths of Rome? Are they lost? Or were they transposed into the most ancient tradition of Annals writing? Perhaps, having been scattered and rivalled by other, better structured traditions, they never did come to be crystallized before the invention of the great political accounts of this small republic that, in the space of two centuries, turned into a vast empire. According to John Scheid,[19] it was writing employed in the service of attempts to master time that led Rome to provide itself with a history and a great tradition separate from orality. A new kind of historicity took shape thanks to the practices of the Roman pontiffs. At the start of each month, standing on the Capitol, they would loudly and publicly announce the date of the nones (the nine days before the ides). Every official announcement involved the intervention of the *rex sacrorum*, the second highest religious figure in the Roman hierarchy. At the nones it was his job to announce a complete list of the month's religious events.

The pontiffs were not only in charge of the time to come that was just beginning; they also exercised responsibility over the time that had past. It was they who preserved the memory of certain things and events that had happened: expeditions of war, successes, defeats, exemplary sacrifices, prodigies of all kinds, and signs sent by the gods. When the year came to an end, the *pontifex maximus* appears to have been in the habit of fixing on the wall of his residence a tablet that listed the outstanding events of the year. This represented a kind of report on the state of affairs between the gods and men. Once the town's bill of health was made public in this way, the pontiff could decide upon the vows and expiatory ceremonies that would best 'inaugurate' the coming year. 'Beginning' the new year completed the task of controlling time that fell to a type of priest who was – as Dumézil put it[20] – endowed with 'freedom, initiative, and movement'. It seems that this half-ritual, half-historiographic activity of the pontiffs, at the intersection of two lunar months or two 'civil' years, prepared the way for the writings of the first annalists and subsequently for historians such as Livy.

In Rome, quite unlike in Greece, the time for human action was strictly ruled by the organization of religious time. But it was Rome, in the wake of the initiative possessed by a pontiff, a figure both religious and public, that, without any reference to tradition or 'the stories of ancient times', saw the start of a historiographical operation with a great future: the telling of the great events of a *nation*, for better or for worse. The events acquired meaning in the context of the way that the year was organized and its place within Rome's long duration over its 'twelve hundred years'. This was a society that felt physically part of its native land but was at the same time intoxicated by 'perspectives of the future that offered progressive gradations of 12 days, 12 months, 12 decades, and 12 centuries'.[21]

The men who were to write the history of the town had inherited all the freedom of the pontiffs, and they were to be neither priests nor magistrates. Historiography in Rome was not a state affair as it was, and still is, in China. In Rome, for all that it was rich in traditions of divination and augury, no system of thought founded upon divination was used to shore up man's control over time or to encourage the progress of historiography. In the Chinese world, in contrast, it was, as we have already noted, the practice of diviners that fashioned a written language, the first system of writing and, at a stroke, established the recording of all that was ritual. The earliest annalists, known as 'diviners', were direct descendants of the 'scribe of divinations'. As either 'historians of the left' or 'historians of the right', to be found in every lordly household, every prince's palace and, later, in the imperial palace itself, annals-writers devoted themselves to keeping meticulous and daily note of the life and actions of their lord or prince and of all his pronouncements and the whole sequence of 'events' that occurred. Within this kind of historicity, which was to prove immensely productive over about 3,000 years, the purpose of an official historian never altered: it was to establish 'whatever each event revealed about the meaning of the general evolution of the world and whatever meaning the general evolution of the world bestowed upon each event'.[22] Time was never under threat from the unpredictable: marked by particular virtues, it unfolded within the order of the cosmos that showed that human nature was a part of universal nature. Why mark out any particular place for human action, within a system in which no event was considered to be unique, unpredictable and new? As Sima Qian, one of ancient China's great historians, wrote to a friend, the purpose of historical research was essentially to 'elucidate the connection between Heaven and humanity through everything that has *changed* from Antiquity down to contemporary times'.[23]

Paradoxically, ancient Israel, which set such a low value on the historian as a particular type of man, deployed a historicity that seems to belie its insistence upon remembering the Covenant between God and his people. Even if the course of events had a meaning and corresponded to a divine purpose that did not seem to favour the creative activity of human beings, it nevertheless unfolded along the paths of the Exodus, moving in a forward direction. The past that moulded Israel into a nation gave it the strength to progress and move on, whatever the stumbling blocks encountered. That past, in the form of a memory of 'divine signs', opened up a breach in time, time without repetition or cyclical closure, and it thereby afforded the actions of men committed to the Covenant a more generous future than that offered by the powerful Office of Historiography that the Chinese set up in the heart of their capital. However rich and complex the writing of history may have been in the Chinese world, it is worth remembering that it was not until 1899 that any reflection emerged there on the dynamics peculiar to history and the necessary construction of a past.[24] Meanwhile, the new Israel, despite an unprecedented sense of history, is making a brutal discovery of the existence of historians and historical knowledge as it reels beneath the impact of twentieth-century modernity.

From the scribes of Crete to the stories of the Amerindians

A few hundred kilometres away from Jerusalem, between the eighth and the fifth centuries BC, polytheistic Greeks were testing out the virtues of alphabetic writing. Prompted, perhaps, by a taste for the unpredictable, they busied themselves creating, in other words founding, dozens, even hundreds of communities all of the same type (*typos*), in the same 'political' form. The Greek gods were completely illiterate and no priestly bodies emerged, so citizens were free to experiment with the efficacy of monumental writing engraved on stelae designed to publicize the decisions that the city reached in its assemblies. Writing was not used to communicate with the gods, as it was in China. When a small city in Crete engaged a scribe to 'write in red letters and be the memory' of the city 'in public affairs, both those of the gods and those of

men', the intention was certainly not to write annals or to establish archives; nor was it to note, word for word, the formulae of
rituals in danger of being forgotten or deformed. The scribe
Spensithius – the date of whose contract is the late sixth century –
set his skills at the service of this Cretan city in order to fortify its
public space and confirm the publicity of its political space.[25]

In particular, the authority of the city was to rest on its written
laws. These fell into two registers: sacrificial regulations or 'sacred'
laws, and strongly worded assembly decisions as to what was hap-
pening and would continue to happen as time unfolded. More or
less everywhere on the shores of the Mediterranean, little groups
of men with a desire to turn their 'us' into a city reaffirmed the
radical nature of what they were beginning. That radicality was signalled in two ways: firstly by the city-founder's recognized right to
act as an autocrat, *autocratôr*. It was a right that was sanctioned and
legitimized by the Delphic oracle, which was, it is true, the independent institution of a god, but of one whose person and history
on this earth inhabited by human beings embodied all the attri-
butes of a human founder. The radical nature of such beginnings
was also indicated by the verb for the action of founding-creating:
ktizein, with its accumulated meanings of clearing, domesticating,
transforming and working on wild and uncultivated land, or, more
precisely, land that was uncared for and empty, *eremos*. The idea of
founding a city emphasized a beginning, *eks arkhes*, from scratch.
In their experimenting with various configurations of politics and
cities, it is fair to say that the Greeks deliberately regarded space
'as empty'. This gave them plenty of room to think likewise of the
present as an open space and of the past as being distinct from the
original times that belonged to the gods. In this way, they were able
to appropriate a close past within a domain reserved for human
enterprises. Much of the historiographical writing in Greece was to
tell of the foundation of cities, making no reference to any religious
or cosmological time, but setting those actions at close range in
secular time.

In order not to seem to be returning to our point of departure
and so as to keep the comparison going, let us cast a last glance
at the Amerindians. At the beginning of the twentieth century,
ethnologists, for the most part Americanists, while building up

collections of native myths, recorded accounts of a predominantly historical nature. Putting together his *Paroles données*,[26] Claude Lévi-Strauss noted that the mythological corpuses of people without writing by and large fell into two contrasting categories: on the one hand, a whole mass of separate, disparate accounts, each with a character of its own; on the other, collections of stories that were interlinked and were oriented towards a past that was not far distant. For the past thirty years, the latter collections of stories have been directly mobilized by the Indians of North America in order to assert their rights over land (in James Bay, the province of Quebec, and British Columbia), within the context of a history moving in to confront the white invaders.

It is within this context of mythologies about identity that, among literate Indians – in the same way as in Kanaka territory and in the African world – a literature is emerging in which great interconnected sets of accounts are combined with others that are selected with a view to validate territorial or even economic and political claims. This provides us with a particularly rich terrain in which to compare different ways of writing history and examine new forms of historicity that are likely to be quite unlike those with which we are familiar in our own Western history. A word of warning, however, to thoughtless post-structuralists: Lévi-Strauss has studied the effects of what he calls myth's degradation into history. He noted the disappearance of stories relating to the creation of the world and also of those that tell of the doings of deceiver-tricksters; simultaneously he noted the appearance of events which, arranged in diachronic fashion, serve to establish a name, a rank and privileges for the figure who is to take central position in the story. This is a particular dimension of a kind of history that is written according to the oral traditions of several families whose ancestors all lived through more or less the same events.

4

The Wide-Open Mouth of Truth

It may be a well-known fact, but it is one worth repeating: our Greeks, ensconced at the heart of a tradition several centuries old, nurtured a sense of the universal so powerful as to offer to conservationists of both today and tomorrow the richest and most widely shared terrain imaginable. Generations of respectful Hellenists have managed to convince the world that the Greeks were the first to develop 'a taste for the universal' and that it was they, basically, who inspired 'the very spirit of our Western civilization'.[1]

In their irresistible ascent towards the Absolute Universal, in the course of the nineteenth century our Greeks were to present evidence of a process considered to be of major relevance to the notion of civilization: it involved a transition from mythical to rational thought, with all its local variants such as the suppression of a global and all-encompassing primitive religion in the face of democratic reasoning and – why not? – the very idea of politics.

As we now return to the themes of 'our Greeks' and the Universal, and 'our Greeks' and the advent of rational thought, we shall certainly do well to engage in some comparative reflection as we reconsider some of the analyses produced amid the fervour of a conquering age.

A return to the 'Masters of Truth'

In the archaic Greece of the first walking statues, paths suddenly opened on to the 'Meadow of Truth', where the Plain of *Aletheia*

(Truth) came into view. Tracks even more secret led to the Fountain of Oblivion or the icy waters of Memory. One day in Crete, the herb-gatherer Epimenides fell into a sleep so deep, so timeless, that he had all the time in the world to speak with Lady Truth in person. In the sixth century BC, Truth or *Aletheia* came to figure as one of the intimate companions of the goddess who greeted Parmenides and guided him to 'the unshakeable heart of the perfect circle of Truth'.

For those in quest of the archaic and beginnings, Truth seemed to offer a fascinating archaeology, ranging from Hesiod's Muses to the daughters of the Sun, the guides of the 'man who knows'. Two or three earlier forays into the notion of the 'daemonic' and the reinterpretations of Homeric and Hesiodic themes in the philosophico-religious circles of Pythagoreanism[2] had already convinced me it was productive to follow the paths leading from religious to philosophical thought. I had begun to examine the subject in a brief article published in 1960.[3] Its starting point was a simple observation: in archaic Greece, three figures – the diviner, the bard and the king of justice – share the privilege of dispensing truth purely by virtue of their distinctive qualities. The poet, the seer and the king all share a similar type of speech. Through the religious power of memory, *Mnemosyne*, both poet and diviner have direct access to the beyond; they can see what is invisible and declare 'what has been, what is and what will be'. With this inspired knowledge, the poet uses his sung speech to celebrate human exploits and actions, which thus become glorious and illuminated, endowed with vital force and the fullness of being. Similarly, the king's speech, relying on trial by ordeal, possesses an oracular power. It brings justice into being and establishes the order of law without recourse to either proof or investigation.

At the heart of this speech, dispensed by these three figures is *Aletheia*-Truth, a power belonging to a group of religious entities who are either associated with or opposed to her. Close to Justice, *Dike*, Truth forms a pair with sung Speech, *Mousa*, alongside Light and Praise. On the other hand, *Aletheia*-Truth is opposed to Oblivion, *Lethe*, who is the accomplice of Silence, Blame and Darkness. In the midst of this mythico-religious configuration,

Aletheia pronounces a performative truth. She is a power of efficacy and creates being. As Michel Foucault would later put it,[4] true
discourse was 'discourse pronounced by men who spoke as a right,
according to ritual'. *Aletheia* and *Lethe* are neither exclusive nor
contradictory in this way of thinking; they constitute two extremes
of a single religious power. The negativity of Silence and Oblivion
constitutes the inseparable shadow of Memory and *Aletheia*-Truth.
In the name of this same power, the Muses, the daughters of
Memory, possess not only the ability 'to say many false things that
seem like true sayings' but also the knowledge 'to speak the truth'.[5]

What place do the sophist and the philosopher occupy in the
lineage of the 'Masters of Truth'? How does their speech differ
from the efficacious speech that conveys reality of the diviner, the
poet and the king of justice? How does the transition occur
between one type of thought, marked by ambiguity and the particular logic that goes with it, to another kind of thought in which
argumentation, the principle of non-contradiction, and dialogue,
with its distinctions between the sense and the reference of propositions, all seem to herald the advent of a new intellectual regime?

It seemed to me that the socio-historical context might contribute to an understanding of the genealogy of the idea of Truth.
During my research on the Pythagoreans, I glimpsed signs of a
process that set in motion a gradual secularization of speech. The
most important sign was to be found in the military assembly of
the Homeric world, which conferred an equal right to speech on
all those brought together there to discuss communal affairs. What
we used to call the 'hoplite reform', introduced in the city around
650 BC, not only imposed a new type of weaponry and behaviour
in battle, more suited to the 'phalanx', but also encouraged the
emergence of 'equal and similar' soldier-citizens. At this point, the
speech of dialogue – secular speech that acts on others, seeks to
persuade and refers to the affairs of the group – began to gain
ground, while the efficacious speech conveying truth gradually
became obsolete. Through its new function, which was fundamentally political and related to the *agora*, *logos* – speech and language – became autonomous, subject only to its own laws. Two
major trends now developed in reflections on language. On the
one hand, *logos* was seen as an instrument of social relations: how

did it act upon others? In this vein, rhetoric and sophistry began to develop a grammatical and stylistic analysis of techniques of persuasion. Meanwhile, the other path, which was explored by philosophy, led to reflections on *logos* as a means of knowing reality: is speech all of reality? And what about the reality expressed by numbers, the reality discovered by mathematicians and geometricians?

Thirty years later, it seems timely to re-examine the assumptions and procedures of that early enquiry and also to consider a number of methodological problems. In 1958, at the Ecole Française de Rome in the Piazza Farnese, where my analysis of the 'daemonic' led me to consider various forms of mediation, Louis Gernet, at my request, sent me his essay 'Les Origines de la philosophie'.[6] For many years I had already been reading the work of this Greek scholar who, in the 1980s, in the shrine of rue Monsieur-le-Prince, was to become the object of some veneration by the devotees of the Centre de Recherches Comparées sur les Sociétés Anciennes and its left-wing historiographer, Ricardo Di Donato, who, with Marxist zeal, travelled from Pisa to organize the liturgy of its 'founding heroes'.[7] In that brief essay – which was very difficult to find until Jean-Pierre Vernant and I republished it in 1968, with other essays, in *Anthropologie de la Grèce antique*[8] – Gernet pointed out the importance of identifying how 'mythical concepts, religious practice, and the very forms of society could contribute to the schemata of fledgeling philosophy'.[9] Gernet paid close attention to the figure of the philosopher, his way of behaving as though he had been 'chosen', and his view of his position and knowledge in the world and in the city. In that same year, 1958, in the Piazza Farnese, as I came to realize the fascination that Greece exerted on ethnology, Claude Lévi-Strauss's *Structural Anthropology* revealed to me new ways of analysing and theorizing 'mythical thought', which Greek scholars hardly dared mention, even among themselves.[10] Underlying my enquiry into the religious configuration of Truth was Ernst Cassirer's and Antoine Meillet's hypothesis that language guides ideas, that vocabulary is more a conceptual system than a lexicon, and that linguistic phenomena relate to institutions, that is, to influential schemata present in techniques, lifestyles, social relations and the processes of speech and thought.

New ways forward

Speech and its use in the early city was my subject then, and my enquiry today continues along the same two general lines. The first concerns the practices of the assembly, which developed out of hundreds of experiments involving models of a political space. Closely linked to this is the nature of the environment in which the many reflections on speech, its effects, techniques and relations with the world and with other people occurred. Currently, I am analysing ways of using speech and modes of behaviour in the assembly from a comparativist perspective, considering Ethiopian communities, Cossack societies and the Commune movement in Italy.[11]

The second line of study follows in the wake of *Themis*, examining schemata of creation and foundation ranging from oracular pronouncements, through the procedures for opening and closing assemblies, to the domain of decisions engraved on stones set up in the unfixed space of nascent cities.[12] Michel Foucault, in his 1970 inaugural lecture at the Collège de France, entitled *L'Ordre du discours* (The Order of Discourse), discovered in archaic Greece the source of our 'will to knowledge' or, more precisely, our 'will to truth'.[13] To me he seemed to be referring to the landscape of truth that my own enquiry sketched in. With hindsight and once we jettison the poorly defined earlier identification of 'power and knowledge', the desire to speak the truth seems to me to have been very marked among the Masters of Truth of early Greece. Such a will or desire is expressed both by the Hesiodic Muses and by the Bee-Women of the young Apollo.[14] Similarly, in the political domain, a desire for effectiveness is always explicit: it is found across the board, from the ritual formula of the herald who opened the assembly with the question 'Who wishes to speak for the city?' to the formula repeated in thousands of decisions legibly carved in stone and carefully positioned where they could be read by 'whoever had the will/desire to do so'.[15] The philosophers wasted no time in attempting to monopolize this desire for truth. But the city was spared such a monopoly, thanks to its use of speech and the practices of the assembly, although this development was, at the same time, altogether in line with the will and desire of those who were obsessively establishing the forms for the government of men by men.

Such an enquiry into not only the semantic field of *Aletheia* but also the proto-history of philosophy and the changes in the archaic world was bound to evoke reactions from the three academic disciplines in a position to judge the validity of the enterprise: philology and history, of course, but also anthropology, if it could overcome its complexes vis-à-vis the other two and their international prestige, in Europe at least. One might have expected the historians to pay some attention to an essay on the 'hoplite reform',[16] but the potential of categories of thought constituted no part of any history programme, whether ancient or more general. Moses I. Finley was wary of anything outside the socio-economic sphere, even politics in the strict sense of the term. Pierre Vidal-Naquet, working at that time with Pierre Lévêque on Cleisthenes and the intellectual transformations accompanying his great political reforms, was the sole exception; I am now even more appreciative of his work than I was at the time.[17]

As for the tribe of philologists, to which, as an archaeologist of the Truth, I am bound to return, it has always fallen into two distinct species: the philologist who thinks and the one who dispenses with thinking. The latter, it must be said, is invariably more prolific, whatever the climate or circumstances, be they those of Vichy or the war against Evil. However, the hermeneutic school of Lille, Germanic and philosophical in its inspiration, undoubtedly belongs to the first species.[18] Won over by a sociology of culture *à la française*, that is to say the works of Pierre Bourdieu, some members of this group of hermeneutists have even manifested an interest in anthropological approaches that may illuminate certain important aspects of Greek culture, such as writing as a cognitive practice and its effects on the modalities of certain types of knowledge,[19] and also earlier work on 'mythology' and 'mythical thought' as it relates to the practices of such an explicitly polytheistic culture from the Homeric epic to almost the end of antiquity.

Tell me, O muse

A recent international colloquium on Hesiod, admirably organized by interpreters of the hermeneutic school, combined philosophy

and anthropology with philology, that most eminent of disciplines.[20] Must an understanding of Hesiod and the Truth of the
Muses really be limited to a 'scholarly study of the works', in other
words, hermeneutics?

I was much affected by the question that Heinz Wismann raised
in his introductory comments.[21] Is it legitimate to apply to the
author of the *Theogony* the modern hermeneutic principle according to which the coherence of the work's meanings in the last
analysis rests upon the autonomous decision of a single individual?[22] The constraints of the principle involve accepting the work
in its autonomy, the coherence of its meaning as a unitary project,
one author at work, and a peerless interpreter responding to
the appeal of that peerless author. Comparison is never even
envisaged – which from the outset discourages any reference to
anthropology, since, as bears repeating, anthropology was born
comparativist. Out of loyalty to its own principles, elaborated
between a reading of Plato and a reading of the New Testament at
the end of the nineteenth century, philological exegesis cannot
accommodate any analysis of historico-ethnographic content.
Institutional practices such as ordeals by water, prophecy via
incubation and Orphico-Dionysiac funerary rituals are barred
from the hermeneutic circle, as are all the representations of
memory and oblivion that throng the cultural field in which
Hesiod belongs. On the grounds that they are 'external' to the
text, Hesiod's text, those 'data' are considered to have no bearing
on the literal meaning that alone gives access to the 'sole meaning'
of the work.

A great deal is certainly at stake here, as is demonstrated by the
state of contemporary 'classical studies' in the United States and
its increasing focus on 'great texts' and their exegesis. For them,
it really does seem simply a matter of maintaining certain privi-
leged values, without the slightest concern for analysing cultural
systems as a way of understanding the mechanisms of human
thought across different cultures. Yet for 'structural essayists', as
for members of the French school of hermeneutics, the subject of
Hesiod's poem is clearly speech – not only its status and authority but also its representation by the poet and the Muses. We all
recognize that from Homer to Hesiod the relationship between

the bard and the daughters of Memory undergoes a transformation and becomes more complex. In the *Iliad*, the Muses are all-knowing and, thanks to them, the poet can see perfectly into both camps. As the servant of the Muses, the bard can recount what happened when the Trojan horse entered the city of Apollo and Hector. Instructed by the Muses, he sings now for Odysseus, now for others, of what unfolds before his blind gaze, as though he himself were present in the days of the Trojan War.[23] However, Hesiod of Ascra, for his part, speaks in the first person as well as the third. An author who is both poet and prophet is present and is chosen by the Muses, who now assume new modalities of speech. Heinz Wismann is right to emphasize this point: 'They say that they know how to say false things [*pseudeis*, which I myself would translate as "deceptive things"] that seem to be real, but at the same time they know how to make true things understood.'[24]

Here the Muses are understood to be reflecting on the subject of narrative and its structures. The order of discourse, *logos*, thus has a double register: one of fine fiction, which is certainly not rejected, the other of 'true understanding'. According to Wismann, this means 'seizing upon the structures of the narrative' or 'the narrative of the true structures', and so on.[25] *Aletheia* thus designates the register of the intelligible, that of true understanding of the work produced by Hesiod and his post-Homeric Muses. I believe that both levels are in the province of the Daughters of Memory, as is shown, importantly, by comparing the representation of the three Bee-Women in the *Homeric Hymn to Hermes*. These Bee-Women instruct Apollo himself – in divination, no less – according to a double register: 'From their home, they fly now here, now there, feeding on honeycomb and bringing all things to pass. And when, sated by honey, they are inspired [*thuiosin*, literally "they leap", like Thyades possessed by Dionysus], they are willing (*ethelein*) to speak the Truth (*Aletheia*), But if they be deprived of the gods' sweet food, they speak falsely (*pseudesthai*) in the distress that assails them.'[26] Here a comparison with the knowledge of a diviner is fundamental; and fortunately for hermeneutics, it can be justified by the definition found in one of the 'great texts';[27] the *Iliad* declares that Calchas is able to speak of the present, the future and the past.[28] In both cases, there are thus two registers: the Bee-Women with Apollo, the diviner, the Muses with Hesiod, the poet and prophet. The difference between them lies in the honey, the means of ecstasy. Hesiod's Muses, more down to earth despite being Olympians, feel no need for ecstasy, not even in the customary form of nectar and ambrosia. The 'desire/will' of the Bee-Women, similar to that of Hesiod's Muses, simply diminishes the mechanical nature of the food of truth and thereby reduces the distance between the two groups.

While hermeneutics may successfully explore the double register of Hesiodic speech, it refuses to make any concessions in the field of memory and oblivion, the ethnographic and religious contexts of which I explored and used in *The Masters of Truth*.[29] A hermeneutist must interpret literally, at the level of words: *lethe* must mean 'a kind of unawareness', the counterpart to *aletheia*, 'the things of which we are no longer unaware'; and this, we are told, means 'we have true comprehension of them'.[30] *Mnemosyne*, or Memory, a divine power married to Zeus, as were first Metis, then Themis, and finally Hera, dissolves into a truly incongruous platitude. She becomes simply 'good memory', because 'to understand *Aletheia*, we must be able to remember what has already been said.[31] Yet the signs provided by Hesiod are certainly clear enough: on Mount Helicon, the Muses are positioned close to the altar of Zeus;[32] they 'fill the poet with breath (*empneuein*), as does Apollo when he gives the elect the knowledge of the present, the past, and the future'.[33] Also in the *Theogony*, *Lethe*, far from being simply 'a kind of unawareness', is just as much a divine power as are the words of deception, the *Pseudeis Logoi*, who are listed among the Children of the Night, along with Sleep and Death.[34] No thoughtful study of speech in Hesiod's poems can afford to neglect the most immediate Hesiodic context, that of 'the work' itself. Similarly, ignoring the Old Man of the Sea, who is listed among the Children of the Deep (*Pontus*), leads one to ignore another essential passage in the *Theogony*[35] and to fail to ponder 'the truth' implied by the king of justice, his prophetic knowledge and his other powers. What kind of 'textual explanation' is it that can, with no justification at all, begin by sweeping whole chunks of the 'work' under the carpet?

The Greeks and us: with or without a context?

Remarkably enough, it has been the American Hellenists at Harvard University, such as Gregory Nagy and Charles Segal, who have paid the most attention to the mythico-religious aspects of memory and oblivion and their relation to blame and praise,[36] no doubt because they recognized the paramount importance of wider horizons of knowledge and were disinclined to consider a cultural system simply as a more or less rich collection of separate and autonomous works. In spite of all the philologists' scepticism, in recent years a number of important discoveries have established the ancient and complex nature of the works and practices of philosophico-religious circles. The first discovery was that of the oldest Greek book, the Derveni Papyrus of around 340 BC, a scroll from the library of Orpheus containing rich philosophical commentaries on the Orphic poems.[37] Next came new gold tablets from Hipponion, in Magna Graecia,[38] and Pelinna in Thessaly,[39] which establish both the 'Bacchic' nature of the initiation reserved for the bearers of these engraved lamellae and testify to belief in a sacred way along which a dead man or woman could pass in order to accede to life in all its plenitude. A kind of Bacchic and Orphic ritual[40] from the end of the fourth century BC in turn testifies to the importance of writing in philosophico-religious circles fascinated by the interplay between Memory, Oblivion and Truth.[41] Finally, on the shores of the Black Sea, at Olbia, a colony of Miletus, excavators of what was then still the Soviet Union discovered bone tablets bearing graffiti from 500 BC. Beneath the three terms *Life-Death-Life* and alongside the words *Orphic* and *Dionysus* was *Truth* (*Aletheia*). On another slender tablet, parallel to the pair *Peace-War* stood the words *Truth-Deception* (*Aletheia-Pseudos*). Finally, on a third tablet, beneath a shortened version of the name Dionysus was inscribed *Soul* (*Psyche*), set close to *Aletheia*.[42]

The philosophico-religious circles of the late sixth century were thus deeply involved with the subject of Truth, the very truth which, rightly or wrongly, Martin Heidegger regarded as the essence of the whole of Greek philosophy,[43] and which was at the heart of philosophical discussion concerning the 'sublation' (or 'overthrow') of metaphysics between the time of the Greeks and 'us'. Few scholars of antiquity or educated readers are aware of how carefully Heideggerians and 'deconstructionists' have built a veritable barrier to separate themselves from the explorations of Greek scholars. Even while Hellenists continue to publish and publicize documents and texts, if not whole works from the diverse world of archaic Greece, they are at fault in not realizing that really the name of the only person who can initiate one into Greek thought is Martin Heidegger. That barrier seems insuperable. Even lucid critics of successive interpretations of Heidegger's views on Truth seem to accept at face value his interpretation of the Truth as the 'unconcealed' or 'de-concealed', making no attempt to 'deconstruct' it or to compare it to archaic representations of *Aletheia*. Admittedly, one of the boldest of those critics,[44] albeit as uninformed as the most obdurate of them about the discoveries at Olbia and Derveni, has written, 'We ought to take a good, hard look at the word *alethes*'. But for Heidegger and his disciples, the history of philosophy and hence the establishment of the meaning of *Aletheia* are part of *the very history of being*. Clearly, this does not make it any easier to initiate a debate on the modalities of 'hiddenness', forgetfulness and memory in Greek culture and thought.

From the perspective that I have adopted from the start, no etymology can be singled out as infallible (thank God). At least from Parmenides on, Greek philosophers recognized that to think it was necessary to debate and argue. When an etymology seems bad or fantastic, no appeal to higher grounds can confer authority upon it. In the context of this enquiry, it is important to remember why the whole field of politics is left out of the analyses offered by Heidegger and his followers, intent as they are on 'overthrowing' or 'overcoming' metaphysics. The etymology of the word *polis* illustrates the point. One fine day, in a seminar, Heidegger said (and was later to write) that the word *polis* comes from *polein*, 'an ancient form of the verb "to be"'. That is an entirely arbitrary etymology. There simply is no convincing and verifiable 'true meaning' for *polis*. Such elementary scholarship was hardly of a kind to check the flights of fancy that followed: the city, the *polis*, if founded on the verb 'to be', itself clearly designated the place where Being is totally unveiled.[45] So it can have nothing in common with 'politics' in the trivial sense of *to politikon*, in Greek or in any other language. So, goodbye politics.[46] The philosophico-religious element was never even mentioned in connection with either the earthly plane or the plain of truth.

It is worth pausing to reflect on this matter since, considering this is a non-debate, the fall-out continues to be considerable.[47] So far as I know, not one of Heidegger's disciples has ever questioned that feeble etymology. A few continue to insist that, for Heidegger, politics cannot constitute a category or domain such as ethics or ontology. 'Politics' – with all its foundation rituals, its gods, and its autonomy linked with so many practices – does not exist. It vanishes into thin air, useless and unknown. Indeed, on closer examination, ever since Heidegger's *Being and Time*, politics, in the now vulgar – even very vulgar – sense, has been heaped with scorn. It constitutes an obstacle to the process of *Dasein*, existence, which is determined by a concern for self that can only be appropriated by turning away from the mundane elements of life and the city with its pointlessly loquacious public places. In this connection, only one philosopher, Dominique Janicaud, braver and more lucid than the rest,[48] has sought to understand how Heidegger's thought laid itself open 'to what happened to him'. I refer, of course, to the recent past, 1933: the philosopher of *Dasein* supported Adolf Hitler's National Socialism, maintained a hermetic silence on the genocide of the Jews, and afterwards failed to produce any philosophical critique of his 'incidental' support of the Nazi party. It may not have much to do with the so very Greek concept of Truth, but it may not be totally unconnected with the equal scorn heaped upon what Heidegger calls 'anthropology'. For his disciples and devotees, the term incorporates the enquiries historians of archaic Greece have conducted both on philosophico-religious circles and on forms of thought discovered through methods that certainly lead neither to familiar places nor to the heart of 'great works'.

The metamorphoses of mythical thought

Finally, two additional matters are worth raising in this retrospective study. The first concerns the 'mythical thought' which, we maintained, in the 1960s and 1970s, possessed a true consistency yet also was 'overthrown'. The second deals with the 'social and

mental' conditions that made possible the deep changes that I
believe to have been detected through studying the history of the
concept of Truth.

First, the matter of mythical thought: in a grudging review of a
work in which I considered the presuppositions of the essentially
Greek category of 'myth', Arnaldo Momigliano[49] noted my disaffection with regard to the question of the transition from mythical
to rational thought in Greece, an issue he considered by then well
established. This historian of history, usually a much more percep-
tive observer, believed that this disaffection indicated a break with
the analyses that Jean-Pierre Vernant had been working on ever
since his *The Origins of Greek Thought*. But Momigliano was mis-
taken, as we all are at times. He had completely misunderstood the
intentions of my book, *L'Invention de la mythologie*, whose real aim
was to reflect on and provoke thought about the category of 'myth'
and its place in Lévi-Strauss's analytic methods – methods with
which I myself had experimented (the first to do so in a Greek
context, I believe) in 1972, in *The Gardens of Adonis*.[50] Momigliano
did not realize that so far had I convinced Vernant of the need to
rethink the category of narratives known as 'myth' that Vernant
himself, with my *L'Invention de la mythologie* solely in mind, had
explained in the popular periodical *Sciences et Avenir*,[51] that 'today,
Greek mythology is changing its meaning'. Unlike Momigliano,
Vernant was not at all upset by this. In fact, at this point, he fully
accepted it.[52]

However, the question here concerns the 'mythical thought'
that was so important in the enquiry begun in 1960. At that time
it was mediated through Louis Gernet, who from time to time
referred to the ideas of H. Usener, but spoke of them with all the
conviction of a disciple of Durkheim,[53] and possibly of Ernst
Cassirer. Cassirer had devoted a whole volume of his *La Philosophie
des formes symboliques* (1924) to 'Mythical Thought'.[54] Following
in Gernet's footsteps, Vernant set up a new 'framework': 'mythical
thought'–'positivist, abstract thought' or, put another way, the
transition 'from myth to reason'.[55] Lévi-Strauss, for his part, had
not yet said enough on the subject. *The Raw and the Cooked*, the
first volume of his *Mythologiques*, appeared in 1964, and it was not
until I was prompted by the comparison between 'alimentary

codes' and Pythagorean sacrificial practices[56] to try new methods of analysing Greek myths too[57] that I saw how new meaning could be given to 'mythical thought'.[58]

In so far as thought of a global nature incorporates a number of different types of experience, mythical thought or 'ancient religious thought' made it possible to elaborate the most convincing configuration of poet, seer and king around a single model of speech with shared gestures, practices and institutions. Now as then, an analysis of the trajectory of *Aletheia* from Hesiod to Parmenides provides a unique opportunity to observe the changes in the mechanisms of the intellect at work in the beginnings of philosophical thought. I am now planning to develop those religious and mythical representations of speech in the direction of *Themis*, positioned between the oracle, Apollo and the assemblies.[59] I have no intention of writing the history of a 'psychological function' such as memory. That is in no way the aim of my enquiry, [60] which is devoted to detecting traces of *Aletheia* in the many places where the tribe of philosophers do not venture. Nor do I intend to seek what might intuitively seem to be *the* hurriedly put together yet definitive logic behind 'mythical thought'. Rather than make the enquiry hang on a contrast between *a* principle of ambiguity and *the* principle of contradiction, I prefer now to emphasize the diversity of the configurations that include the figure of *Aletheia* and the *comparison* that should be made between the orientations of the various frameworks encountered during that first reconnoitre. Perhaps it is no longer enough to know that Truth, too, has a history and that, once Parmenides had depicted the Goddess as revealing the Way of Truth to him, Truth had to be proved, argued and put to the test of refutation.[61]

From the time of my earlier enquiry into Truth and its double registers to my comparison between different ways of beginning – the central theme of *Transcrire les mythologies*[62] – I have chosen to concentrate on instances of rupture and radical change. My reasons for doing so were twofold. The first reason, explicit and factual, is that the Greek data are full of clear-cut beginnings and sudden impulses, of which the Greeks are acutely conscious, thanks to the very force of reflection that fuelled so many new kinds of knowledge. The second reason has become clearer in the course of my comparative studies: conditions that involve profound change and abrupt breaks with the past make it easier to select apt comparisons between cultural systems. In the case of the Masters of Truth, the comparison remained internal: between two types of men, two successive configurations, two models of speech. Between Hesiod and Parmenides, the determining factors seem to have been the passage of time and changes of context. I wanted to analyse the social and mental conditions of the transformation of truth between Epimenides and Parmenides. Simply noting that there was a discontinuity seemed unacceptable, particularly since the contrast between two models of speech, the 'magico-religious' and the 'dialogue-speech', became explicitly clear at the point when Greek cities and their culture first appeared. What I then called the 'process of secularization' was first manifested in a social framework whose practices and representations, so important in the formation of the city, were found described in Homer's poems, particularly in the *Iliad*. Now more than ever, the assembly practices and the representations of space that made for egalitarianism in warrior circles, which are described in epic, seem to me to be essential for an understanding of the increasing importance of the *agora* in the first Greek cities of the eighth century as well as for the development of the model of *isonomia* in the 'political' world of the seventh and sixth centuries.

In the variegated landscape of the transitions from 'mythical thought' to the 'positivist and abstract thought' that were underpinned by the mental outlook of the city, a definite lesion was immediately visible. With this rift came a different kind of speech, a different framework, a different kind of thought; and this rift occurred within a sharply defined time-frame (the Homeric eighth century; the mid-seventh for the qualitative leap represented by the 'hoplite reform'; and between the two, the first circular agoras laid out on the ground by the founders of the Magna Graecia cities from about 730 on). These matters are worth following up and keeping under observation, even today, however hard it is to do so. With the advantage of hindsight, I will refrain from again speaking of 'undeniable connections' between a major phenomenon such as the 'secularization of thought' and changes as rich and complex as 'the emergence of new social relations and unprecedented political structures'. Given the scarcity of evidence in archaic Greece, it was tempting to make too much of the coherence between widely differing aspects of the culture and boldly to connect them with a network of interrelations between social and mental phenomena that were extremely diverse and in many cases barely possible to detect.

In a careful and intelligent analysis of the Masters of Truth, Maurice Caveing[63] has pointed out the large gap between a kind of egalitarian and secular scene and the formulation of, or at least insistence on, a principle of non-contradiction in the field of Parmenides' *Aletheia*. It was, to be sure, somewhat cavalier to pronounce upon what quite a few earlier scholars had solemnly defined as 'a great social fact'.[64] At the time, its importance was not in doubt and any attempt to qualify it would have seemed quite incongruous. The forms and processes of the legal and political practices of the two theories or parties between which a choice had to be made are certainly worth investigating. All the same, it does seem more justifiable to stress the role that the technique of mathematical demonstration may have played in sixth-century Greece, together with the insistence on non-contradiction within this new kind of knowledge, as Caveing did in 1968.

The debate on 'common matters' (*ta koina*) within a sphere of equality is not necessarily directly related to the debate between intellectuals on the rules of reasoning, the forms of demonstration, and the criteria of conceptual analysis.[65] Indeed, the recent comparativist studies of Geoffrey Lloyd[66] have revealed the complexity of this laboratory of new rational thought with all its various types of knowledge, its competitive frameworks of rivalry, its different types of proof, and its ways of distinguishing between discourse that is true and discourse that is not. In any project involving an increasingly refined comparison between modes of reasoning and ways of formulating or establishing the truth, there is, even today, a place for the Masters of Truth.[67]

5

'Digging In':

From Oedipus of Thebes to Modern National Identities

'Digging in' may not seem a very Greek idea, at least not one as obviously Greek as myth, mythology or mythography, let alone 'democracy' or 'politics'. In less colloquial English, perhaps the most relevant and evocative term might be the 'stock' (*souche*, in French) from which 'rooted beings' spring. But there is something to be said for the expression 'digging in' when it comes to a comparative attempt to set in perspective whatever it is that smacks of those Athenians who proclaimed themselves to be 'autochthonous' (*autochtone*, in French). The term 'autochthony' entered the language of the Ile-de-France in 1560, even before the terms for 'natives' (*indigènes*) and 'aborigines' (*aborigènes*) began to circulate, spreading from the earliest colonies. In the Greek spoken in Athens, the word meaning 'autochthonous' did not appear until relatively late, around 460 BC, at which point it may have been one of the numerous coinages of the tragic poet Aeschylus.[1]

The word 'autochthonous' carries an earthy ring and a gravitas. The claim of those said to be autochthonous is that they are 'born from the very earth on which they stand'. And the French, for their part, readily identify with the image of springing from such ancient stock. However, 'digging in' as a translation for the French *faire son trou*, with its evocation of both effort and depth, helps us to see autochthony in perspective, primarily in relation to founding and ways of doing this. The French word for hole (*trou*) is an old one, said 'to go back as far as the language of one of the peoples that occupied Gaul before the Celts'.[2]

That brings us quite close to the time of Aeschylus. But *trou* or hole is the word used for a cavity, natural or otherwise, that might provide shelter for an animal or a man – not that hole-dwellers should, on that account, leap to consider themselves automatically promoted to the status of autochthony if not of ancient stock, for to do so would leave out of account the dynamism associated with the effort of digging – digging out something rather bigger than a hole, indeed not so much a hole but rather a 'territory', a word that can likewise be associated with animals as well as human beings. The notion of establishing a territory or, as the anthropologists say, 'territorializing', opens up a field of comparison so extensive that, without needing to turn to philosophy for an answer, we might just as well simply ask: 'What is such a place? What is such a site?'[3] The first thing to do is *observe* the ways and practices involved in creating territories in Japan, in black Africa, in Mesopotamia, in the Tuscany of the Medicis, in Magna Graecia, in modern Israel and – why not? – in the Athens of Aeschylus and Euripides or the mythological Thebes of Cadmus and Oedipus. We must observe and compare how societies imagine and picture what it means 'to be there', to inhabit a particular place, found a site, move from one place to another, in short all the possible ways for the human animal to 'dig in', to plan and organize the portion of living space that he needs or thinks he needs in order to survive.

Consider the tribe of Hellenists, for example. Metaphorically speaking, they tend to believe themselves 'autochthonous', sprung from the very earth of those Greeks whom they regard as 'incomparable'. Theirs is a twofold yet altogether limited autochthony, inward-looking and also, in many cases, obtuse. This is proved by the extraordinary distance that the most scholarly of the tribe maintain in order to keep the claim of the few to be born solely from themselves separate from what happens everywhere else in the world, with all its diverse ways in which to found or create new places. In circles dedicated to 'the encouragement of Greek studies', that is to say, Hellenist circles, there have been, on the one hand, those specializing in autochthony, the noble – in other words, Athenian – section of the Greek world, and, on the other, experts on Greek so-called 'colonization', all those foundations elsewhere: on the shores of the Black Sea, in Sicily, in the

Mediterranean, and in the Magna Graecia of the 'landless', the rootless, the exiled. So it has been hard to show, or rather to detect that 'founding' intersects with autochthony,[4] and that in order to become 'indigenous' it is necessary to acquire roots and be labelled 'native', if not 'aboriginal'.

Becoming aboriginal

Step slightly aside, and the question 'How does one *become* autochthonous?' looms. Let us, for a moment, leave our Greeks who proclaim themselves to be 'born from the very earth where, clearly, we have been forever' and follow in the wake of the subjects of Her Majesty the Queen. The British possessed excellent ships and controlled most of the seas and oceans. One fine day in 1788, a few of them planted their flag on a land now known as Australia. On the shores of New South Wales, they proceeded to establish a splendid penal colony. Foundations come in many guises. The explorers of a previous expedition had spotted through their telescopes only a few scattered groups of 'savages'. No large settlements, no indication of agriculture (and the British, especially when at sea, are extremely conscious of how much a landowner loves to cultivate his land). No sign of herding or trade or of the roads indispensable for it. There was only one conclusion to draw: this was the kind of land well known in learned circles as *terra nullius*, land belonging to no one.[5] The indigenous people scattered throughout New South Wales – thus renamed without their knowledge – were now called aborigines – an etymologically dangerous move, for *ab* means 'since the beginning'. We all know what happened later. Ever since the land-claim of 1981, two centuries later, Australians have been trying to rewrite Australian history, with their busy lawyers deep in negotiation with the lawyers of the autochthonous people of Australia who, for many years now, have no longer been living as hunter-gatherers.

What the telescopes of the British did not reveal or even hint at, around 1788, was that the local aborigines were one of the races most fanatically attached to the land where they were born, but attached in a quite different fashion from that customary in England. In every part of what was now called Australia, individuals personally possessed places, recognized as sacred, that they passed on to their descendants. Some might say that these were places with which those individuals simply identified. But that would be over-hasty, for different societies produce different kinds of landowners and different links with the land. Today, in various law courts, including the High Court, the matter is being bitterly debated: if the link with the land is of a religious nature and not a matter of 'property' (in the legal sense), is it still a link? This is an ongoing story that anthropologists, as well as lawyers and all claimants, are busy recording. What is the meaning of a 'primordial' right over land that, for the past two hundred years, has been owned by colonists established around the penal colony? This constitutes a remarkable field of observation to which I urge the specialists of Athenian autochthony to flock, along with historians of anciently rooted European stock and American nativists: for what is on show is the forced, as it were 'forceps' birth, of aboriginality. The primordial natives have to prove their link with the land on the basis of genealogies, customs and institutions. In an Australia where some people have been born aboriginal, it is infinitely less simple to be 'autochthonous' than in a fourth-century Athens where all that was necessary was to be told that one was autochthonous and to repeat this every evening before sitting down to supper. 'With different times come different customs', as the saying goes. But what *is* the Australian nation? Certainly a nation in crisis. For its native historians are writing a history that resolutely begins 60,000 years ago and is based on the testimony of palaeontology and archaeologists.

The paucity of Athenian autochthony

To move from Australian aboriginality to Athenian autochthony takes but one, short step. What did becoming autochthonous in the Periclean sunshine involve? Nothing simpler: all you had to do was listen to the established deliverers of funeral orations, an earlier and more modest version of the history professors of nineteenth- and twentieth-century nations, officials trained to swell every breast with passionate national sentiment. All it took was one century – roughly from 450 to 340 – of self-adulation, with its own stereotyped ways of persuading the most illiterate inhabitants of the outbacks of Attica that they belonged to an autochthonous race: they were the only real men on earth, born from that earth on which the inhabitants had remained, continuously the same, ever since the very beginning.[6] This was a land blessed by the gods and handed down by ancestors: a heritage, a legacy transmitted in a direct line from the past. Meanwhile, indispensable contrasts were provided by collections of immigrants' cities composed of foreigners, and towns put together out of the scrapings from the bottom of barrels of every kind.

Clustering around the first-born from an idealized bloodless mythology, the Athenians postured as pure autochthonous beings, confident that they had been polluted by no drop of foreign blood.[7] Yet only one century earlier, Solon 'the lawgiver' had been encouraging all the residents and immigrants of Attica to become citizens of Athens; and by the time of Themistocles and Salamis, that is to say in 480, Athens regarded itself, with equanimity, as a troop of armed men ready to board a fleet of two hundred ships and weigh anchor for Sicily, where it would found an entirely new city.[8]

As a result of looking at autochthony purely through Athenian eyes, some Hellenists have managed to, so to speak, totally forget the rich mythology telling of the founding of autochthony in Attica itself. Elsewhere I have drawn attention to this and twice analysed it in considerable detail. All to no avail: no come-back at all.[9] No surprise there: all eyes are fixed on Athena; Poseidon remains ignored, despite the fact that he is solidly established within the Erechtheum, at the heart of the Acropolis. For Poseidon, the god with the trident, was the first to arrive, as soon as he heard that there was a post going as a 'poliad' deity in a land that was unpromising but had good access to the sea. However, it was the second to arrive, Athena, who assumed the place of the primary deity of the future city, while Zeus solemnly swore before the committee of enquiry that he had in no way favoured his daughter, his 'motherless' daughter. After a little while, Poseidon had returned, passing by way of Eleusis, for he was duty bound to come to the aid and support of his son Eumolpus. War ensued between Eleusis and Athens, war that Athens did just manage to survive, but only by involving Poseidon, Athena's rival. After witnessing the death of

his son Eumolpus, the god who, in the past, had made a gift of the
sea to the aborigines of Attica, now fell upon Erechtheus, the king
of all the Athenians, both female and male, and thrust him down
into a deep crevice that had opened up at the centre of the
Acropolis. There, in what was known as the sanctuary of
Erechtheus, the great god was every year solemnly worshipped as
Poseidon-Erechtheus, the Poseidon who had violently buried in the
earth the first being to be called autochthonous by the Elect of the
Ceramicus: a fine example of firmly rooted autochthony, well and
truly founded, deep in the earth. Take my word for it: among
Apollonian architects, Poseidon's reputation as the god of founda-
tions was thereby firmly established.

Non-autochthony at Thebes

Founding and autochthony intermingled in a pool of blood, at the
feet of Cadmus, on the site of Thebes. This was also the city of
Oedipus – but not the Oedipus of the psychoanalyst's couch or of
the mythology that Freud inscribed upon the sands of the subconscious. This Oedipus was the one who was born defiled into a nexus
of defilement that seemed to regenerate itself endlessly.[10] Cadmus
could do absolutely nothing about it, for it had all been set up by
Apollo. From Delphi and its mouth of truth Cadmus, who had
journeyed there to discover what had become of his sister, the
beautiful Europa, received his marching orders: he was to found
the city of Cadmus, unknowingly slay the angry son of Ares, and in
that very place sow in the furrows of the earth the teeth that would
grow into the first-born of Thebes. These would spring up fully
armed and would immediately slaughter one another, just as, in
their turn, would Oedipus' sons, Polynices and Eteocles. Those of
the first-born of Thebes who survived did so only to pass on the
defilement. In the city of Cadmus and Oedipus, autochthony and
founding combined to produce a history full of murders, defilement, bloodshed and irredeemable debt. In recent years, certain
bronze tablets discovered in Selinus have informed us that in
Greece some ancestors were pure, others impure but purifiable.
However, the ancestors of Oedipus and Laius were impure
through and through: nothing and nobody could wash away or

obliterate a defilement that renewed itself spontaneously, just like the mythical olive tree on the Acropolis of Athens. This founder chosen by Apollo in his sanctuary at Delphi was doomed to an autochthony of blood and death.[11]

How did one become autochthonous? In various ways, as we are beginning to see. Some founders rooted the first-born of the land in its soil; some, who set off to found a city in virgin soil, saw autochthonous beings springing up from the earth; others, who were completely nomadic, such as Herodotus' gentle Budini, simply declared themselves to be autochthonous and nobody took exception to this. Doing anthropology *with* the Greeks does not mean setting up, in some corner or other, a little typology of local autochthony or an exportable concept of founding. Forgive me for repeating myself: comparativism *with* the Greeks or others involves *raising questions*. What do we mean by 'autochthonous' or by 'aboriginal' or by what we call 'founding'? And what is meant by those who declare themselves to be 'genuine, real autochthons', sprung from land whose inhabitants have remained the same ever since the beginning? This is not at all what 'indigenous' meant as used by Rabelais, who had in mind people who had lived for a long time in a particular region and who, among themselves, liked to call themselves a 'country'. The tone is quite different when those from outside find words to designate the original inhabitants of a country taken over by colonizers.[12] The Arabs of Algeria were said to be autochthonous neither in the nineteenth century nor for long after.

And when the Dutch of today choose to call foreign residents in Holland 'allochthons', they are introducing a notion of autochthony that is neither that of the small assemblies of Athens nor of autochthony as seen by the Indian tribes of North America.[13] How disconcerted the violent early twentieth-century 'natives' of white, Protestant America would have been to discover, in the midst of their own 'nativism', that elsewhere, in the State of New York, they were regarded as 'autochthonous' by its earliest colonizers! Comparisons between different periods can be as stimulating as those between societies very far apart spatially that are unaware of each other; and I believe that involvement in comparisons and in the art of constructing comparative possibilities should encourage us to take a further look at our own categories and notions: for instance, the notion of 'founding', which masks that of 'digging in' and the latter's comparative potential. Let me return to an analysis of the spectrum of possibilities:[14] 'for us', does 'founding' not evoke the singularity of a space that has its own particular name, characteristics and limits within a vaster area; and does it not furthermore suggest a point in time that is a beginning in a history, a particular chronology, a particular historicity and, along with all this, something like an initial, isolated, recognized event of a striking or even solemn nature? A founding seems to presuppose a significant starting point from which a historical process can develop. Finally, when we think of 'founding', we have in mind an action involving particular gestures, a ritual or ceremony inseparably associated with some individual who selects this spot as the apparently unique place in which to put down roots. Autochthony, on the other hand, does not particularize space; neither does it appear concerned with a starting point in time. The first-born of Athens was no Romulus, but was associated with the idea of a birth from its very earth. For that idea and its perpetuation, the essential factor lay in its 'sameness', the unchanging nature of that earth, but at the same time in a decisive and constitutive *exclusion*: the exclusion of others, which does not seem immediately implied by the concept of 'founding' itself. An autochthon with an iota of self-respect would not allow himself/herself to be confused with just anyone, male or female, who happened to have lived in the region for a long time. He/she alone (like Euripides' unforgettable Praxithea) was autochthonous. All the rest, to put it bluntly, were hybrids, half-breeds, immigrants, aliens.

How to be national

Incomparability is an essential condition for autochthony. That is why autochthony provides such a useful guide to the ways of 'digging in' and constructing majestic monuments and prestigious architectural creations that then confer upon the landscapes of our great nations their most striking features. As the reader has no doubt guessed, the subject to which we are leading is that of our 'national histories'. The first question was: 'How to be autochthonous?' The next – as our Greeks have indicated – is 'How to be *national?*'[15] How does one become national? Presumably, different ways of 'digging in' stem from different mythologies. On these matters, the Greeks seem to be good, as it were '(electronic) conductors'. How does one become national, how does nationalism come to the surface out of a combination of history, mythology, and identity cards and documents? These are all questions that testify to the fertility of an approach that draws comparisons between them and us, or between ourselves.

Admittedly, at first sight, a nation, with its high legal profile, seems a far cry from the parochial arrogance of the autochthony of a mere village. For an observer of humankind, who must be a born comparativist, the most precious asset in the world is freedom to move and look around, wherever one chooses: to the other side of the Alps, for instance. In comparison to France, Italy seems to provide an example of a national community somewhat uneasy in the face of its own past. Nevertheless, in the eyes of an anthropologist, whether close or distant, it is in the so very diverse Italian peninsula that it is possible to observe an autochthony in the making, an autochthony that is of a local nature but that manifests in miniature all the features of a great nation of pedigree stock on a European scale.

As we all remember, 1989 saw the destruction of the Berlin Wall; but it also witnessed the creation of a Northern League, soon renamed 'Padania' [i.e. northern Italy].[16] An astonished world learnt that in the silty land of the god Po, the Padans, just like the Sioux of the Smithsonian Institution, had been invaded by foreigners who stole their land, of course, but also their customs, their way of life – all the richness of what we nowadays label their 'ethnicity'. That is what foreigners tend to do, especially those who invented 'colonization', both the word and the thing itself. Within the space of just a few years, an ethnic group until then unknown – no doubt it had been reduced to silence – proclaimed the startling strength of Padanity. These people were pure Celts, born free, who, throughout their long history, had never experienced the gangrene of central authority in the state mode. Thunderstruck, Italy discovered that it had harboured a proud and free minority, 'pure Celts', who had victoriously weathered the long winter of occupation by a 'southern majority', which had lasted ever since the disaster represented by Rome and its tentacular empire. Here then was yet another ethnic group, but this time one of the most rare purity: for it had been preserved by the inaccessibility of the places in which the best of its members had taken refuge, to wit, wonderful Alpine valleys, today peaceful and profitable 'memory sites' opened up, following the French model, to cultural tourism, which, thanks to the gods of Europe, has become the foremost industry of not only France but Italy too. As the true Padans quickly spotted, within the present context of successive waves of foreigners, the recurrent threat of Islam, and continual aggression perpetrated by the centralizing state, it was urgent to create a 'Ministry of Cultural Identity and Memory' that would define the criteria of the Padanian identity and, with the aid of historians and anthropologists (the alliance is highly recommended), would promote the recognition of 'a genetic heritage indissociable from its *cultural patrimony*'.[17] The creators of Athenian autochthony were amazed. Well, this was fine work . . . Now Wallachia, which has claimed to have been founded by Philip II of Macedon and will soon be tracing its roots back to Orpheus, the Rhodopian bard, has recently despatched a mission of enquiry to the Mantua region. And Wallachia, home to now urbanized transhumant shepherds, has quietly, for the first time ever, been recognized to possess a cultural identity of its own by the European Community, which is well aware that Europe is not only a huge market but also a great institution devoted to the cultivation of a multitude of cultures.[18]

We must continue to compare and experiment, always asking what? and how? Our project should now include an investigation into what is implied by *national*, for there are many ways of 'digging in'. What should be the focus of an investigation into nationalism in the manner of those devoted to 'founding' and 'being autochthonous'?[19] The nation? Nationalism? Both are clearly too cumbersome, with too many semantic strata. Before settling on our way of approach, it may be helpful to examine some of the ideas of modern sociologists grappling with practices that seemed to them part and parcel of the concept of 'national' of the years of their youth. Norbert Elias, the author whose thinking in the 1930s produced *La Société des individus* (*The Society of Individuals*), remained

virtually undiscovered until fifty years later. Elias was in a position
to observe at first hand how individuals proclaim themselves to be
members of a nation by adopting a series of practices that are
inspired or dictated by the State, and how, within just a few years,
they totally internalize the values and norms of the Nation-State. A
practical *habitus* creates a sense of 'nationhood'. A little later, Ernest
Gellner, in Oxford, in a book, *The Construction of Nationhood*,
which tends to focus on France more than England, suggested a
theory of nationhood. In 1905, Emile Durkheim had called nationhood 'an obscure, mystical idea', being convinced, for his part, that
because a 'nation' is a unique entity (although surely there were
already a whole clutch of them apart from France . . .), it constitutes an unsuitable subject of study for a sociologist since its very
uniqueness excludes comparison. Nevertheless, Gellner was unde-
terred: according to him, the nation, which he took to be a fundamental social entity, was born in modern industrial societies at the
time of the appearance of strongly structured states whose economic growth required a homogeneous culture. Resources were
centralized by the state, which then set up an educational system
that imposed upon every individual a standardized literate culture.
Gellner's outburst reveals the flimsiness of his thesis; for it thus
turns out that what is known in France as the *thèse d'Etat** shapes
the nation and produces nationalism in a variety of forms.

Your papers, please!

All that we can glean from sociological thought, so little given to
comparison, is that certain practices constituting a *habitus* create
an artefact; and there are, or may be, certain practices that are more
likely than others to produce a sense of nationhood. If we give up
the idea of comparing so-called 'national systems' directly, how
should we set about analysing those practices? I suggest that we
focus on a number of practices essential in the construction of an
identity, specifically those materially required for a national identity. This may lead to the discovery that what is central to any
nation-with-historians-of-its-own is a mythology, a *myth-ideology*,

* Translator's note: the *thèse d'Etat* is the dissertation submitted in order
to be awarded an advanced academic degree.

in short, whatever possesses the power to generate belief in a 'national history' of a unique and incomparable nature.

Why choose identity rather than essence or uniqueness? Because, clearly, a search for identity requires one to turn out all one's pockets. Do great countries suffer identity crises? How can one 'identify' foreign cultures that are irreducible to our own modes of thought without destroying the specific originality of those other cultures? Might it not be the case that only a native, an autochthon of a particular culture, has the right to speak of its identity? Anthropology has encountered and confronted these questions raised by the ambiguities of the word 'identical'. If one says *idem*, 'the same', one has to ask 'the same in what respect?' In the way that articles that are perfectly similar are identical even though distinct? Or the same as in 'unique' – even if they are perceived and named differently?

What is the position of the identity of Wallachia or that of France? Is it a matter of an identical personality or of things that are said and considered to be identical? These days, cultural identity has a ministry devoted to it, and soon there will be many more of these. Well, that's as may be. For my own part, I have chosen to tackle the matter of national identity (a nebulous notion) by way of *administrative practices and procedures*. What I have in mind is an individual's official status, the formal establishment of citizenship through the practice of issuing certain cards, even a national identity card[20] (a particular feature of Europe, or at least of France). Here are some dates and points of reference. The law of 2 March 1848 established so-called 'universal' suffrage; but what is the definition of a French citizen? In 1789, individuals were lyrically identified with their country in song: 'Aux armes, citoyens!' But ballot boxes are not a matter for improvisation. Who was who in 1848–9? No doubt official registers did exist, but were they carefully kept up to date? Did they stem from some central authority? The answer is no, so how could X or Y be identified, given that the only technique known to the police consisted in simply looking people over in order to pick out individuals who had been found *guilty of some crime*. Up until the 1880s, everyone could treat his/her past as he/she wished. The identification revolution – which is once more in action – began with Galton and fingerprints:

a physical sign was taken from the individual's body, making it possible to identify every separate human being. Alphonse Bertillon, the super-policeman who had shown the nation and the republic how to identify each human being, was put on show in the Universal Exhibition of 1889, as living proof of 'the French genius'.

As soon as photography appeared on the scene, the police force took good note of it; and it also kept a close eye on the progress of statistics and physical anthropology. The identity of an individual could be constructed from a certain number of indicative features or signals: the shape of the nose and the ears, the colour of the eyes, bone structure and physical peculiarities. Identity was now submitted to identification, particularly in the cases of dangerous individuals, those arrested, those found guilty and persistent offenders. More often than not they were regarded as aliens, for the latter were naturally individuals who were suspect as they came and went within the national territory. Identity through identification was initially applied not to citizens but to 'others', while citizens shared an abstract right to 'national sovereignty'. Along with identity through identification, the notion of 'nationality' traced a demarcation line separating foreigners from those called Frenchmen. For Littré, in 1866, nationality was represented by gatherings of people of the same race or nation and to take a country's 'nationality' was to adopt the customs of that people or nation. Those were the days . . . Twenty years later – after the 1870 war, when Lavisse was already at work writing *The History of France* – there was no longer any question of an individual taking a new nationality. *Nationality*, like identity, had become negative; it marked out foreigners, who could not be employed in public posts such as medicine (a regulation that was maintained in France right down to the early or mid-1990s). Foreigners could no longer be 'nationalized', although they could be 'naturalized' and thereby granted *some* of the rights of the country's 'natural' inhabitants.

In the period between 1900 and 1930, immigration was intensive in France: according to Dominique Schnapper, it accounted for 40 per cent of the population – a fact that makes it easier to understand certain nationalistic obsessions. The matter of so-called universal suffrage returned to the fore along with the practices designed to establish identity: the *elector's card* in principle became compulsory only in 1884, forty years after the proclamation of universal suffrage in 1848. But what was the use of an elector's card in the absence of a national identity card? Despite all the efforts of the police and the Ministry of the Interior, so many difficulties were raised that such a thing was not created until 1917, in midwar, and again it was intended *solely for foreigners*. In 1946, a national identity card became compulsory for all 'natural' citizens. A 'national tyranny' had developed; the declarations and laws by which it was accompanied in France, throughout the nineteenth century, have been carefully recorded by Gérard Noiriel. It was a process directly relevant to any understanding of the emergence of the genre of 'national history'. A comparative history of, say, national 'tyranny' in Europe, the United States, and other parts of the world where nations and nationalisms first appeared, would no doubt shed welcome light upon the art of writing history in the nationalist mode.

How to be a 'pedigree' historian

This is really still the same terrain in which we encountered the autochthony of the Greeks, as we sought to understand the meaning of 'digging in'. Through these digressions by way of identity and identification, I am trying to suggest that the reason why the framework of 'nationalism' is so solid and so resistant is that it is constructed from excellent materials and put together by highly qualified workmen. Indeed, I salute the historians of France writing between 1850 and the present day, those who produced the *Histoire de la nation française*, the *Histoire de France* published in 2002, and *L'Identité de la France*, published in 1986. I salute them as I would have saluted our Athenian orators of funeral speeches and national ceremonies celebrating the dead. As the reader may already suspect, I am hoping that an analysis of these various microconfigurations will prepare the way for a comparative study, first in the extensive strata of the European Continent, but elsewhere too, in Hindu and nationalist India and in a Japan that is locked into a hypernationalist insularity to which its local historians, anthropologists and archaeologists are all expected, as in duty bound, to contribute.

Comparison, setting things in perspective, setting oneself in perspective: such exercises are poles apart from the genre of 'national history'. My hypothesis, which I hope to test with the aid of my collaborators, is that national history becomes established in parallel to the definition of an identity indicated by official documents and papers of the 'identity card' type.

It is time to tackle the subject of *history, mythology and myth-ideology*. How does one come to belong to a nation? How does one become a Serb of Greater Serbia? We appear to be well informed on the subject, thanks to historians every bit as critical as those who showed us, in the case of Israel, how pedigree Jews were formed. In Serbia, both the spade-work and the finishing touches were provided by the ideologue-academicians of 1875, the historians and literary writers of 1912 and 1913 and, later, the 'Memorandum of the Serbian Academy' published in 1986. This document claimed to establish the historical rights of Serbia. In response to the 'scandal' that it caused, Milósevíc said and wrote: 'Is there any people, any state in the world with any pretensions to wisdom that would be ashamed of its own Academy?' The whole file of evidence was published and translated by the courageous Grmek and his collaborators in a work entitled *Le nettoyage ethnique* (Ethnic Cleansing),[21] at a time when the purity of Serbian blood was spattering Kosovo and leaving other Europeans dumbfounded.

As far as I know, there have been no historians working alongside anthropologists who have suggested a comparative study of a range of microconfigurations in order to reveal how the history of the Germans, the French, the Italians, the Serbs, the Croats, and even the British and the Americans has been written over the past century. *Englishness* was invented between 1880 and 1920, and historians contributed generously to its creation, as they were clearly duty bound to do. However, can there be any historian, be he/she American, English, Spanish or Italian (not to mention French), who was not startled, as I, a naive reader, was, to discover that it was possible in this day and age (to be precise, in 1986, but republished in 2002) to write that 'a historian can only be on a completely firm footing with *the history of his own country*'.[22] In other words, only a 'pedigree historian' – I do hope the vigilant shade of Marc Bloch can hear me – is capable of instinctively understanding the 'original characteristics', meanders and detours of France. 'We must not allow our history to be expropriated' was the theme with which one great historian (an illustrious academician whom some of us used to see in a quite different light) harangued his fellows: Fernand Braudel, no less, in his last testament, *L'Identité de la France* (The Identity of France).[23] I hope not to be reminded, yet again, 'But after all, that is not all that he has done', even if it is, happily, true. National historians across the board have vouchsafed not a word on the matter. I have yet to read a *critical* analysis of this work that defends the idea of a France that existed before France and even goes so far as to speak of a national neolithic period and to whisper that France was a land promised to the French as early as palaeolithic times.

However, to return to the present: in April 2002 it was claimed that this France had been rediscovered. In the second round of the presidential election, shockingly, the extreme right – 20 per cent of the citizens of France – propelled Le Pen into second place, overtaking the candidate of the left. Panic ensued. In the aftermath, opinion polls announced that *30 per cent* of this same French tribe declared themselves to be 'in favour' of the National Front. Was that really so strange? Not if you take a glance at *Les Origines de la France*, produced by the 12th 'Colloquium of the Scientific Council of the National Front, October 1996', published in 1997. In this document, the historians whom Jean-Marie Le Pen had gathered together cited *our* Greeks, now Plato, now Aristotle, without realizing that the founder of the Lyceum was what the Greeks termed a 'metic'. Enthusiastically, they went on to copy out commonplaces produced by a number of compliant academicians of both sexes. And these same theorists of a 'rediscovered France', the illustrious Robichet and the scholarly Mégret included, dredged much of their material from the last work of France's great historian, Fernand Braudel, for it had shot straight into the ranks of the classics, unrevised and with no purgatorial delay. The work was, of course, *L'Identité de la France*[24] – 'long-term history' (*histoire de la longue durée*), so how could one complain? and with the same old foetid stamping ground, that of national history. Worldwide, we should do well to recognize the professionals of national history when we see them.

'Our' national mythologies

In the Europe of 2005 and the Europe of twenty-five nations, I believe that the exercise of comparison has both intellectual and civic virtues. The field of enquiry is not hard to mark out: its aim would be to compare various species of the 'national history genre' and analyse in context the elements that compose the myth-ideologies of nationalism in twenty-five colours and a thousand and one shades. For example, what form of authority is credited to the historians, schools of historians, academy or academies that lay claim to, or indeed possess, what they sometimes call 'sovereignty'? The Académie française claims *sovereignty over the French language* and, these days, that claim is recognized and sanctified by a *Journal official*.[25] In the comparative studies that I have undertaken in the company of colleagues working in both history and ethnology (to give them their disciplinary labels), we have tried to see how 'the dead are treated' in societies ranging from those of Africa to those of the ancient world and including India and contemporary Japan. 'The Earth and the Dead' is more than the slogan launched by Maurice Barrès; it evokes a whole agenda: starting from the dead, you can construct a pattern of ancestors, and this may take many different forms. And on the basis of ancestrality you can proceed to historicity which, in turn, opens up a wide field in which to place different modes of historicity in perspective.[26] Without comparison that encompasses societies that are far distant from one another in both time and space, there is a danger of remaining confined within *a single national framework*, as is shown by the philosopher Paul Ricoeur who, convinced that historiography is rooted in the cult of the dead, has declared 'We are in debt to our dead': that is to say, 'our dead of the Christian West and those who believe in that'. But what is the significance of the dead in, say, China, with its two thousand years of history and historians so very different from the emulators of Lavisse? It is only from outside, from afar, that the peculiarity of the tradition that encompasses Le Pen and Barrès becomes noticeable. Left to himself or in the bosom of his family, a historian steeped in the history of France will not even think about it, so heavily does nationalism weigh upon him, preventing him from seeing, or rather from thinking, beyond this, his natural, maternal, communal framework (I use the term 'communal' in the sense in which it is applied, in France, to national schools, the *écoles communales* in which France's children are all nurtured – or at least were up until 1970).

To speak of myth-ideology or national mythology may seem lacking in respect for all the historians who devote their lives to publishing and interpreting written documents and increasingly complex vestiges of societies now lost in time and perhaps in space too. And indeed, I should not have ventured to do so had I not come across the label 'National Mythology', announcing – yet again the example is French – a vast work that is the latest product of what is known as *la nouvelle histoire* (new history). I refer to the *Lieux de mémoire* (Places of memory), edited by Pierre Nora who, on page 7 of the quarto edition (1997), writes as follows: 'What we must do is set in place and analyse the most weighty blocks of our representations and our *national mythology*.' This is a serious matter, and a chorus of his peers in France took up the cry: how to set about writing the history of Padania? . . . Sorry, I apologize for that slip of the pen; what I meant was the history of France at two removes and explicitly defined as a great 'national mythology'. It was as I had suspected ever since the publication of the first volume. 'The history of France' genre or that of national history, with all its pomp and circumstance, is bound to stem from myth-ideology. Any history of Germany before Germany, Italy before Italy, or France before France from the outset postulates the greatness of its mythical origins. The belief that its identity has been unique in its unbroken continuity ever since the beginning rules out the slightest mention of anything that might cast doubt upon this incomparable phenomenon. But let the Academy speak for itself: Academician René Rémond, welcoming a new member, Pierre Nora, congratulated him on his 'stroke of genius' in 'leading us back to face *the mystery of our national identity*' (the italics are mine).[27]

In this national business in which history and mythology are intertwined, *identity* seems to have constituted a guiding thread ever since Michelet – where France is concerned – right down to post-Braudel, by which I mean the *Histoire de la France* edited by Jacques Revel and André Burguière. Their introduction reminds the reader of Michelet's unforgettable founding remark: 'France is a Person'. That remark, along with others no less memorable belongs to what these two authors call 'our historiography' – the historiography by which the Ecole des Annales modestly swears.[28]

France-the-Person, or the personification of France, provides identity with a noble dimension, and Revel-Burguière strike out, in the first edition (1989), as follows: 'We have a crisis of historical identity' (here, in France, clearly).[29] It is up to historians to react to this, starting from the contemporary situation. I again quote Revel-Burguière: 'Our point of departure has been the *singularities* that today characterize the French identity, so that we may endeavour to rediscover the *original* characteristics of the national make-up in their origins and to trace their transformations.'[30]

Throughout all five volumes, the key words stand out: 'identity', 'singular' and 'original' characteristics, and anything that can be regarded as 'national'. It is of course by no means the first time such expressions have been used to fashion a 'national consciousness'. All the same, what a strange project it is that tries to start from the peculiarities of an identity that has been so fundamentally fashioned by the *genre* itself that it cannot bring the latter into question. It is as if it were impious or blasphemous to take apart a history that is guaranteed by nothing but itself and can apparently only be told from within. Fernand Braudel puts that point even more strongly when he says – and again I quote him: 'A historian can only be on a completely firm footing with the history of his own country.' It was certainly he who won out over Marc Bloch in the *Annales* school. I in no way misrepresent him when I call him 'a pedigree historian' (*un historien de souche*) and stress his affiliation (spiritual, of course) with Barrès and his *La Terre et les morts* (The earth and the dead). 'To make a nation,' wrote Barrès (using a formula that would be excellent for a comparative approach), 'you need a cemetery and the teaching of history.' One century later, Braudel, in his *L'Identité de la France*, was evoking 'our dead', our dead ever since palaeolithic times, who are present beneath the feet of the living;[31] 'our' territory (with all the 'attachments' that others have listed) is nearly two million years old, twenty thousand centuries. In circles close to Braudel, it is said that this is a grandiose, *'longue durée'* (long-term) view, while Revel deems it *à propos* to stress that the *Annales* have always taken an interest in national history.[32] So it is easy enough to believe that history means getting the dead to speak, along with Michelet and a number of others; that to write history is to acknowledge our 'debt' to the dead, as Ricoeur declares, with Braudel emending that to *'our dead'*. In this respect, he distinguishes himself from Michelet, who was well aware that there are *also* dead in Germany and in Spain, and that in some of the provinces over which France reigns national hegemony merges harmoniously with a 'foreign genius'. As no one would deny, with Lavisse history became increasingly national and increasingly less comparative. Of course, that is a truism, but it is apposite at this time for those (myself and others) who wish to use comparison to dismantle the national histories that are so crushingly present in this European space within which all thought begins and proceeds on the basis of the concept of nationality. For it is certainly high time for us to dismantle them and set about analysing them by studying some of their microfigurations.

Finding good material to compare

We must compare, but how? If 'digging in' seemed to present a good angle from which to start, it may be useful to return to the specific procedures of a comparativism that is both experimental and constructive, carried out by anthropologists and historians working together (even if, in this particular instance, I myself seem to be assuming both roles). This is a comparativism that is bent on constructing genuine comparabilities. As can be seen, my intention is not to set up a typology, nor to propose a morphology of either founding or autochthony. I have allowed myself to slip from 'How to be autochthonous' into 'How to be national', a matter that, as I see it, seems to lead to three interlocking notions: the writing of history, the mythology that pervades it, and the formation of an identity that creates nationalism. I am convinced that there are many topics that afford opportunities for experimenting and constructing comparabilities, which is why it seems to me necessary to work together, in collaboration. But right now I think that one of the most productive approaches might be to follow the guiding thread of identity. Following along the track leading from a person in a place to the individual identity card held by the citizen of a nation will lead directly to the major practices and interactions of what constitutes nationalism.

The myth-ideologies that form the framework of the histories of nations and their identities are complex, and to analyse and compare them it may be useful to follow paths that are signalled by such pairs of key terms as 'the Earth and the Dead' or 'Blood and Earth'. In Europe, such words clearly have an almost mythical quality: the dead, our ancestors; the earth, the soil, the motherland; blood, an inherited life, a sacrificed life. Earth seems to constitute an extremely general category and it is easy to get lost once it becomes 'the inhabited world' or the earth as a whole. Yet if you turn 'earth' into 'a place', it on the contrary becomes a very subtle concept. 'What is a place, or site?' we have asked ourselves above, or, to put that another way, 'how *does one make a territory*'? This line of questioning soon leads in at least two directions: one being, 'What does it mean to start something, or to inaugurate something, to write its history and give it a historical perspective?' This directly involves what is known as historiography. The other direction involves questions such as 'What does it mean to be born from a place, to be a native, indigenous, aboriginal, with or without roots?' Of course, a place is not only a piece of land; it may hardly be a place at all, when one is stuck in the angle of a window for instance, or perched up a tree, or when the soil of a place is stuck to the soles of those constantly moving about in what is professionally known as a 'hunting ground'.

Wherever you look, you find particular practices; for example, all those surrounding 'How should we treat the dead?' Bury them, burn them, leave them for the birds, eat them, trample them underfoot, never mention them aloud, remember them three times a day, forget them, deliberately or involuntarily? There are so many possibilities, so many that have been observed or are observable and that wrest us out of the torpor of a one-track mind induced by the single meanings of Barrès and his heirs. The fields for comparativists are countless, with layers that could be provisionally mapped and celebrated with some glasses of champagne shared by historians and ethnologists working together. Consider Switzerland and Israel, for example. Reliable observers of humankind have noted certain peculiarities of Switzerland as a nation, a nation-state. In the first place, there is not a trace of citizenship before about 1813 or 1815. 'Nationality' itself dates from 1891: a date to be remembered, for it was then that the state made the sovereign decision to date its foundation to 1291. In Switzerland, the Switzerland that made that backward leap of six hundred years, there are now four professorial Chairs of national history, located, of course, in four different cantons.[33] For how long has national history been written? Is the vision or version of it produced in Berne the same as that produced in Lausanne? Is this a unique case in the archives of historians and ethnologists? Let us consider a few other examples of identity and national history. Take a glance at the United States, where each state decides upon its own version of a frequently conflictual past, even if this is less rich in centuries than the past of Helvetia (Switzerland) or, of course, France. What does 'to die for one's country' mean in Valais, and in Geneva? Curiously, the natives themselves do not seem to have much to say about the ways of writing the history of the Swiss state. What a pity.

The invention of the pedigree Jew

Israel, as a state, is even more recent. But there, critical history has pursued its enquiry, making no compromises, to the sound of a whole battery of bulldozers, dynamite and mechanical diggers. The myths created, barely half a century ago, around the roots of the Jewish state from the time of the 'Yichouv', the embryonic Jewish state, have been carefully scrutinized. The state is small, but the laboratory that it offers comparativists is one of the best equipped in the world. Many experiments have been carried out by the natives; those most recently undertaken should prove useful to both observers of humankind and comparativists. The land from biblical times down to present-day Israel is the focal point under the most active scrutiny in the myth-ideologies of the Jewish world. How to treat the dead? How to treat the land? As mentioned above, in Australia the High Court is investigating the bitterly debated question of links with the land. If they are of a 'religious' nature, as the aborigines maintain, rather than a matter of 'property', in the Anglo-Saxon sense, can they still be regarded as *links?* This is an excellent question for Israel, for it encompasses its nomadic beginnings and all the ambiguities of what was said (but at what cost?) to be a Promised Land. The new Palestinian Jews, who claim to be Hebrew, have no wish to remember the exile; whereas the virtuous orthodox Jews continue to live out the exile in the Holy Land itself, in expectation of redemption. If I had to cite but one book on these themes, I would choose the excellent *Israël, la terre et le sacré* (Israel, the earth and the sacred) by Attias and Benbassa, which deploys a wide variety of versions elaborated over close on three thousand years around the question 'What makes a (particular) *place?*'[34]

Let me recall a few contrasting images without pausing to consider the details of their contexts. First, the fact that, in the Bible, a bible for nomads, people on the move, pasturing their herds in the desert of where other people live, land is something that is bought, a plot here, a plot there, for a tomb, an altar, or perhaps a tent for Jacob. The tribe's angry and possessive little god is loath to become the god of a particular holy place. He persists in residing in a portable Ark rooted nowhere, insists on living in a tabernacle made of canvas and animal pelts, but nevertheless exalts that which is *sacred*, sacred and exclusive. In the Old Testament, the only portion of ground known as 'Holy Land' is situated deep in the desert, in a burning bush where the god of Israel made his presence manifest. Here is another powerful image for comparison: the Promised Land is a land already occupied by other chosen people, but unworthy ones that it has spewed out, for they have defiled it; and before long the god of the Covenant will be shouting at the new inhabitants, 'This is *my* land, and you are just foreigners living in my place'. The Promised Land was promised by a god 'without land', and it is he who is the god of the Book for the Jewish diaspora, landless for so long. Do the schools of Israel teach children that Palestine was under Arab-Muslim rule from 634 to 1099 – almost five centuries? I imagine not, no more than they explain how so-called 'holy places' come to be invented and by dint of what practices and what mystical representations both past and present. For archaeology comes to the aid of the notion of nationality in Israel, as it does in a number of other excavation sites where people seek to root an autochthony that can so quickly become alarming.

It is not just archaeologists; geographers, too, are at it. In 1870, France-the-person was 'amputated', losing Alsace-Lorraine, Lorraine which had been 'reattached' in 1766, according to Barrès, the man 'with roots' (although not many people now remember that). In 1903, led by Lavisse (him again!), professional geographers were busy identifying extremely ancient places where men had established links with nature very long ago; soon they would 'demonstrate' that each of those places possessed a physiognomy, a personality that set it quite apart from anywhere else. In Israel, after the Six Day War, a new myth-ideology of the land began to grow, that of the Jewish 'natives' (the *sabra*, a word derived from the Arabic for 'cactus'), Hebrew Jews crossed with imaginary Bedouins. The Bedouin was praised, the Arab rejected. Zionist historians of the early 1930s had begun this work, seeking to demonstrate that there could only be one nation on the soil of the land of Israel (a land where, it is worth noting, it is not the dead who do the rooting) and insisting that the most specific characteristic of Israel was its *particular historical consciousness*. Its historicity stems from the Holy Book; never mind if, as Revel and Burguière's *Histoire de la France* claimed, history was first and foremost a French passion, thanks to the teaching of French local history. Vichy France did not need to create a Ministry of Cultural Identity and National Consciousness. Instead, it chose to encourage French ethnography, shoring it up with physical anthropology that would be extremely useful to the 'racial dictators' of the near future, whose prime mission would be 'to purge the French nation'.[35]

I was keen to undertake a comparative exercise – on my own in this instance, but with collaborators elsewhere – in the field of *nationality*, because this is the area where, especially in Europe, over the past century and a half, history and its historians have been setting up fortresses and bastions of scholarship centred on one single artefact: the nation, along with all that the concept of nationality invariably excludes, starting with hundreds, indeed thousands of other cultures that are declared to be foreign and, by and large, 'uncivilized'.

Analysing the components of these myth-ideologies of identity ever since those autochthons in Greece, and producing hypotheses as to the relations between the choices and orientations that render some of these national myth-ideologies more effective than other less robust ones – all of that, I readily admit, constitutes part of the 'useless knowledge' produced by the human sciences. But what would be directly *useful*, in this day and age, would be to undertake a radical critique of the histories of identity that are inherited and developed more or less everywhere in Europe, in the first instance by politicians, historians and the worthies of a right wing that has never been worried by its extremists. Experimental comparative work of this kind reveals that the Emperor has no clothes – and a good thing too. It also encourages debate relating to the responsibility of those who sanction or themselves write this type of autistic history – just as if we are still and forever in need of the old 'necessary lie' of which Plato spoke: a tale of an exclusive autochthony, in other words a potentially lethal identity.[36]

6

Comparabilities Viewed from the Vantage Point of Politics

In the United States of Europe and of America, it is widely believed that democracy fell from the skies once and for all, to land in Greece and even in one particular city there, Pericles' Athens. Since the eighteenth century, the interpretation of other, more revolutionary beginnings has repeatedly proceeded by way of dialogue with that city. In the memories of Europeans, inaugurations of democracy hold an important place. The Italians like to look back to the communal movement of the twelfth and thirteenth centuries; the English, the first to dare to behead a king, are happy to contemplate their House of Commons, while the French, with good reason, set a high value on the radical break constituted by 1789. All these national traditions are respected, if not respectable. They belong to the Europe that is in the making; and the historians of its various nations have certainly not failed to show that they deserve respect, even as they carefully eschew comparisons, which, as they see it, are not necessary, given the differences in chronology. Besides, comparisons might offend national memories, over which, above all in Europe, the writers of history naturally take it upon themselves to mount vigilant guard.

Multiple beginnings

As a result, more often than not historians of politics, closely followed by political theorists, limit comparisons between ancient and modern democracies to value judgements, the most popular of which leads one to wonder whether the Athenians did *really* experience true democracy. For it is Athens, preferably the Athens of Thucydides, that seems, in the course of barely two centuries, to have become the sole example worthy to enter into dialogue with the 'real' democracies that – God be praised! – have colonized both sides of the Atlantic. As everyone knows, or can easily find out, in the space of two centuries, between the eleventh and the thirteenth, the beginnings of the communal movement in Italy mobilized dozens of towns; and in ancient Greece there were several hundreds of small human communities experimenting over more than three hundred years with a would-be egalitarian form of politics. In Tuscany and Venetia, even the smallest communes engaged in an adventure that involved making choices that would carry them into a history of their own. And likewise, from the eighth century BC onwards (just yesterday!), each of those tiny cities in Sicily or along the shores of the Black Sea set about inventing their own ways of deliberating and deciding upon 'common affairs'. The little town of Draco and then of Solon – I mean that village-Athens of modest beginnings – represented but one type of city among dozens of others, all enjoying the same freedom of creating their own completely new practices of communal living.

Comparison, but not of a parochial kind, is an immediately effective way of escaping from the claustrophobic sense of being trapped between an endless 'Greek miracle' and an incurably obese 'Western civilization'. For thirty years now, the field of comparison has been expanding to include other societies and new continents.[1] For example, historians of Ukraine and the Russian world have rediscovered the surprisingly 'democratic' manners of the Cossacks of the fifteenth to seventeenth centuries.[2] Meanwhile, anthropologists who went to southern Ethiopia to investigate kinship systems there, have been bringing back in their nets a whole haul of autochthonous assembly practices that mark out 'places for politics', as Marc Abélès, one of their discoverers, has called them.[3]

Even without waiting for the discoveries of other observers of human beings – who tend today to be very anxious not to be accused of ethnographic harassment – it seems fair enough to note that such 'places for politics' have been invented many times over in societies widely separated from one another by both time and space. The Ochollo people of the Gamo mountains, who have been living in southern Ethiopia since the nineteenth century, do not, so

far, appear to have consulted the communal archives of Siena or
Arezzo; nor did the fifteenth-century Cossacks of Zaporoia necessarily discover from the *Iliad*, let alone from the site of Megara
Hyblaea in Sicily, the principle of the *agora* and the circular community assembly that dates at the very least from the eighth
century BC. As for the French members of the Constituent
Assembly of 1789, although they were relatively well informed
about the English system that had been in place for several centuries, they seem to have had to and wished to invent everything
themselves, from scratch, on the more or less tabula rasa left by
what would soon be called the *ancien régime*. From historians who
are liberated enough not to bother about the constraints imposed
by the order that governs them, anthropologists have learnt that
certain cultures in both Africa and the Slavic world have, both in
the past and in contemporary times, set in place forms of 'democracy' in assemblies convened to debate the group's 'common
affairs'. It is about time that we recognized that there was no more
a Greek or a Cossack miracle than there was an Ochollo one.

Places for Politics (with a capital P)

Politics and *places for Politics*: it is commonly believed not only that
both the abstract notion of politics and concrete Politics one fine
day fell from the heavens, landing on 'classical' Athens in the
miraculous and authenticated form of Democracy (with a capital
D), but also that a divinely linear history has led us by the hand
from the American Revolution, passing by way of the 'French
Revolution', all the way to our own Western societies that are so
blithely convinced that their mission is to convert all peoples to the
true religion of democracy.

I have always, both here and elsewhere, made my filial respect for
the 'tribe of Hellenists' very clear, and it is on the strength of that
respect that I have endeavoured to learn more about a number of
the beginnings among the hundreds of little cities that emerged
between the eighth and sixth centuries BC.[4] But all the same, it has
to be said that from one continent to another (for Hellenism is both
universal and 'catholic'), there are distinguished historians, acade-
mics and scholars in the strictly Teutonic mode who continue to

argue, now courteously, now pugnaciously, about . . . what? The invention of Politics, in Greece of course, but above all about its place and date, day and hour of birth, the colour of its eyes and the nature of its sex – for the latter is a major question of interest on our university campuses, since in France we use the masculine noun, *le politique*. *'To politikon'* is a false neuter inherited from the Greek language into which it appears to have been introduced by a lecturer visiting Athens from Halicarnassus, by the name of Herodotus.

No sooner did I perceive the status of this question than, as a precautionary measure, I hastened to take my leave of *the* Greek city, without wasting time or paper making an inventory of all the fashionable expressions in which the subject has been decked in Munich, the Latin Quarter of Paris and Cambridge, to cite only the smartest houses of high fashion. Of course, I, like anyone else, have chanced upon people who will declare to all and sundry that all societies are political, that politics means power, and that everything always starts with distinctions drawn between friends and enemies. But I could see no reason, on that account, not to wipe the slate clean, or almost clean, in a word, not to reject all ready-made definitions of Politics.

The will to assemble

Wipe the slate clean? How clean? Leaving only the practices of assembly, in particular practices observed in situations where such an institution is still being initiated so that, with any luck, those practices take simple forms. What I am talking about are practices of assembly or, more precisely, practices associated with a will to gather together, *a will to assemble*. That is the first point. But assemble in order to do what? To *discuss common affairs*. That is the second point, but it is not an innocent one, for I have found it necessary to make a very specific choice. This is not a matter of gathering together for a fishing expedition or in order to barter feathers for claws. I realize how very porous and insecure the apparently firmest frontiers can turn out to be; but a definition such as procedures involving words used to express an idea of 'that which is common' can perhaps delimit a provisional context for this 'will to assemble together', a context within which something like politics or even 'a place for politics' may be constructed. As can be seen, this kind of comparativism is 'experimental'.

I think that the advantage of this deliberate choice of the concept of 'a will to assemble together in order to discuss common affairs' is that it provides an initial category within which to begin to work that is flexible yet not too fluid. This is not a general paradigm such as, for example, the 'civic humanism' or *vivere civile* that historian John Pocock proposes – a set-up with a prince as political agent, surrounded by his home-grown Florentine associates: the citizen, the orator and the inspired legislator. That concept may, to be sure, serve as a way to penetrate the post-sixteenth-century Anglo-Saxon world, but it is as unexportable as the category of 'empire'. Comparativists who are mistrustful of 'homologies' should shun like the plague such entries in so-called encyclopaedias of the social sciences. Let me appeal to the impartial observer (for they do still exist): is it not the case that 'the will to assemble together', as described above, is neither a category that is too local nor a notion that is too general, of the 'catch-all' type?

The category selected for an enquiry published in 2000[5] thus led directly into a series of questions relating to concrete practices. Who sets in train the process of assembling together? Is it just any member of the group? Or is it an elder, a man with authority, an elected leader? Or an individual endowed with religious powers? Where is the assembly held? In a place that changes from one assembly to the next? Or in a place that is marked out, a fixed venue specially arranged or even architecturally designed for the purpose? Are rituals associated with this place? Discreet rituals? Solemn ones? Who opens such an assembly? Who brings it to a close? Who presides over it, and how? Is it preceded by a smaller council meeting, or not? If the former, what type of council? Is there some kind of agenda? How does one gain the right to speak? By making some gesture? What gesture? If there is an argument, what form does it take? Does it involve contradiction or not? What about the assembly calendar: are the assemblies held at regular intervals? Is this will to assemble urgent or calm? Does the assembly come to a final decision and, if so, how? By acclamation? By a show of hands? By secret voting? By a majority vote? What is the status of the minority? Does the assembly need a quorum in order to operate? What proportion of the total membership of the assembly or the community does the quorum involve?

As co-operation between ethnologists and historians progresses, the more the questions become precise and the more differences proliferate, much to the benefit of the experiment. As can be seen, the important thing is to encourage reflection upon the complexity of the structure of something that could be called 'politics'.

The other advantage of the approach via a study of 'the will to assemble together' is that it allows one easily to acquire a perspective on a whole series of societies as diverse and as far-flung from one another as the Italian communes of the European Middle Ages, the Buddhist monasteries of Japan, the members of the French Constituent Assembly, the Cossacks who lived at the time of Machiavelli's *Prince*, the Ochollo people in today's Ethiopia, the Circassians of the last century, the Senoufo of the Ivory Coast, the (to use La Fontaine's expression) sleek, plump secular canons of the medieval West, the tiny cities of Magna Graecia and Sicily – in short, a whole gamut of cultures mobilized in the course of the first stage of a collaborative investigation: twenty societies studied, not in general, but as micro-configurations analysed by researchers working from within, many of them for as long as twenty years.

Let me repeat: in this company, I have never stopped learning. The first thing to do was to sweep one's desk clear of heavy kitsch knick-knacks such as the concepts of the state and democracy that are on offer in every supermarket catering for the human sciences; next, purge oneself, morning and evening, of all fantasies concerning origins; forget, however hard it might be, the primordial hordes represented on celluloid by one's favourite films; close the cupboard door on the Holy Family of one's Western, if not Indo-Aryan childhood; be done with the reign of a primeval human 'community', that matrix born at the world's dawn directly from nature or – worse – 'produced by the hands of God', as Tocqueville (yes, Tocqueville) used to say.

Comparing beginnings

Start with simple forms, observe the practices of beginnings, work on micro-configurations, for they are easier to compare as 'comparabilities' than complex or semi-complex states stiffly hemmed in by their macro-configurations. To be sure, beginnings take multiple forms and are widely diverse. They come about sometimes in a virtually empty space, on a tabula rasa or a levelled foundation flush with the ground, sometimes in highly sophisticated contexts. From one society to another, the birth-pangs of what we might call a 'place for politics' are never the same. For the first Cossacks, self-proclaimed free men, all there was before them was the steppe and its icy silence. For all those Lilliputian cities traced out in the sands of Magna Graecia, there was, to begin with, virgin land which, at first sight at least, seemed unoccupied. For the revolutionary Pisans of the 1080 Marine Commune, there were, on the contrary, already the town, its nobles, the imperial authorities and, closer to home, the Church authorities. Facing the members of the French Constituent Assembly, as they tried to convert their semi-circle into a full one, there was what would soon be called the *ancien régime*, the king and a hierarchical society of orders and privileges to fall upon and dismantle with hammer blows.

Let us keep an eye on those members of the Constituent Assembly, those mutants of 1789. For that was a fascinating beginning that is easy to observe. From the springboard of its formidable 'will to assemble together' to discuss the affairs of one and all, it proceeded passionately to invent a series of assembly practices and to dream up a new kind of space for permanent deliberations between 'the nation's representatives', each of whom, in principle, held an equal right to speak on everything that concerned the welfare of the people – the people who were soon to be consecrated as sovereign. Along with a multitude of new practices, there emerged ideas expressed by a number of different voices on the subject of a new kind of place for politics that recognized no precedents. The virtue of such beginnings is that they reveal how configurations take shape and what elements combine to produce the idea of a community, ways of organizing a kind of group-sovereignty, of mentally structuring a public space, and elaborating a type of citizenship.

Far-flung comparison constitutes an intellectual game that affords one the pleasure of collaborative, unhurried experimentation. To provide the reader with a glimpse of what it involves, let me convey

a bird's-eye view of some of the factors that it has proved possible
to compare within the vast domain of 'Who wishes to speak?' (the
title that we chose for our comparative enquiry because it seemed
to echo the formulaic demand of a herald opening an assembly in a
Greek city). The simplest way to do this is to put together a collection of notions that seem to operate as good litmus-papers in the
field of 'the will to assemble together' for clearly defined purposes.
Let us focus on three such notions: the notion of 'public matters' or
communal affairs; the notion of 'citizenship' (in inverted commas);
and, finally, the pair constituted by 'sameness-equality'.

On public matters

If one selects for special study the theme of the practical ways of
assembling together, one has a chance to observe how the representation of communal affairs may be affected by the practices that
stem from a local will to assemble together. A will: let us pause to
consider what this implies. People may simply flock together or
they may be assembled; for example, a chieftain or a minor royal
may order them to assemble. Sometimes people flock together of
their own accord, when something unexpected happens, when
there is an accident, when something surprises the passers-by. They
are told to keep moving, that there is nothing to see. But the will
to assemble together for precise purposes is never anything but the
work of a minority, an active minority. What motivates such a
minority? Without necessarily expecting a satisfactory explanation, let us rephrase that question in terms of certain types of men
who carry more influence than others.

I chose the formula of a herald of antiquity not because it is
Greek (for no one could accuse me of Hellenomania), but because
it introduces a 'will' without which this particular kind of politics
– one kind among others oriented towards the debate of public
affairs, could neither be instituted nor expand or develop. To have
a place reserved for the discussion of affairs that are *common* to
individuals who are, of their nature, different and spontaneously
unequal may seem a strange idea. The 'will to assemble together'
appears to impose itself progressively through the adoption of
practices and a kind of setting that reveal to the group something

like the beginnings of sovereignty for the group over itself. For the people engaged in this work – work that is quite taxing – discussing affairs said to concern all, speaking of what is felt and recognized to be most essential to the group involves them in finding new representations, which they do by all adopting particular practices and making use of convergent forms of symbolism.

A place for politics or a place of equality in the making may seem pretty unremarkable. Let us pick out one group at random: secular canons used to be expected to discuss common affairs together three times a week. They elaborated a fair system of remuneration to compensate for the considerable inequalities between them. But the *universitas*, the name for whatever was common to these secular clergy, was strengthened by the choice of a central meeting place, such as the bell-tower of a particular hall for the use of citizens and townsfolk might be.

The *universitas* of the canons included a coffer for the storage of archives and a seal that conferred a measure of authority. The Cossacks, whether from Zaporoia or from the area of the Don river, certainly did not meet twice or three times a week; however, they did observe a far stricter equality that initially covered every domain of activity: warfare, hunting, fishing and the cultivation of the land. The whole community (*tovaristvo*, in Ukrainian) was present here. It existed not only when all the Cossacks formed a circle several ranks deep in the main square, but also when the mace of the military leader, the seal of the judges, and the great silver inkwell of the secretary were deposited at the centre of the assembly.

To represent and symbolize 'that which is common', the earliest Greek cities had the idea of, not money or a sacrificial altar, but a public hearth in the guise of Hestia – a common hearth corresponding to the Romans' Vesta. This embodied the idea of a united city in the place where, on a daily basis, the magistrates in charge of communal affairs congregated.

In medieval Japan, the meetings of Buddhist monks took a different form. The assembly was preceded by an oath of union and harmony. Each man present was in duty bound to tell the whole community all that concerned 'each and every one of them', and an assembly that regarded itself as unanimous considered that its decisions and judgements were passed with the gods as witnesses.

In the eyes of those monks, the force of their decisions was greater even than the will of the imperial court. In the land of the Senoufo of the Ivory Coast, at the heart of the space reserved for the egalitarian assembly of initiates, one place was left vacant for 'the Old Woman', and it was from this that speech for all was delivered. In France, Ledoux, a visionary architect at the time of the Revolution, wanted to set up an Altar of the Motherland, bearing the inscription 'Die for Her' at the heart of the semi-circular National Assembly that was also the heart of the nation-motherland. This would have been a political place that could not have been more highly charged.

On Justice

As I made my way between such rewardingly contrasting cultures, it occurred to me that 'Justice' would surely not be an incongruous category in the formation of what we shall now continue to call a 'place for politics'. Let us put out of our minds villages of Europe where the separation of powers is part and parcel of the native landscape. Can there be places of equality or places for politics where the institution of justice is not an essential requirement? Justice for the people in this place who consider that in some respects they are all 'the same' and equal, rather than subjected to one another or linked together by an inegalitarian system of kinship and obligations. Progressing along quite different paths, societies that know nothing of one another may all come to discover that a relationship of justice between people who are equal and similar is by no means irrelevant to the constitution of a political link. To put that more simply, it seems that communities that aim to establish a kind of sovereignty over themselves tend to confer upon themselves the authority to rule upon what is just and what is unjust. Such a community must set up 'courts', choose judges and create juries, for one of the first tasks of a deliberative and executive assembly might well be to set in place one or more courts to judge crimes involving bloodshed. Whose blood? That of a new 'citizen' or blood shed by a member of the community or by a stranger or even by the 'local people' who inhabit the space that the new collectivity has made its own and considers as the land over which it, as a community, exercises authority. It would seem that in these circumstances, homicide is regarded as a direct attack upon the community as a whole; and it is the community that then constitutes itself as an assembly of judgement, opening up a space in which all the 'citizens' gather together to form what we would call popular juries. One of the most decisive actions in relation to communal affairs and the solid establishment of an initial city might be to invite all the citizens to set themselves up as a single jury. Visiting Philadelphia in the course of his travels as an observer in America, Tocqueville expressed his astonishment at the admirable invention of popular juries, for, as he saw it, this implied that it was the greatest number that established the *truth* in a public affair. This matter seemed to him to involve the very right of suffrage within any political order seeking to emerge in the mid-nineteenth century AD. For the Cossacks, free men and warriors, the seal of justice was one of the three symbols by which the community declared its presence and recognized itself to be a community. In the world of the Italian communes, notaries and jurists at an early date pronounced upon justice in matters concerning the *universitas*. I am told that in northern Italy, Milan for example, the space devoted to 'citizens' justice' is in many cases more ancient than that set aside for deliberative assemblies.

More needs to be said here. The exercise of justice for the commune or the city contributes strongly to the promotion of the autonomy of common affairs. To be more precise, justice can help to distinguish certain characteristics of an individual within the circle of the 'citizen body'. With the advent of criminal responsibility, individuals learnt to free themselves from 'family solidarity', wherever that still festered. Each individual now proceeded to become a legal subject within the space of courts that took into account not only public accusations but also argued defences. At this point a body of law took shape, which distinguished between different degrees of responsibility and fixed a suitable scale of penalties to accompany them. For those 'wishing to speak' and for the political coming-to-be of a citizen in that particular place, this was, I believe, an important step leading towards the creation of a fair-minded individual, that is to say, one called upon to pass fair judgement upon his 'equals' and those 'the same' as himself.

Citizenship in the making

A second notion that may also prove to be of practical use is that of 'citizenship', an excellent litmus-paper in the field of political potentials. For example, all you need to do is determine what are the qualities that are desirable or required for those bent on assembling to speak exclusively of common affairs. Within the circle where the question 'Who wishes to speak?' is asked, who is this first orator? What must he be? What must he have? How can he claim to be qualified? For example, the 'equal rights' of citizens decreed by the French Revolution had no meaning outside the philosophical context of the eighteenth century. But what was the actual meaning of 'the right to equality' when the Declaration of Human Rights was proclaimed and published, against the background of the dissolution of a regime according to which the privileges granted to the various social orders depended on their hierarchical rank? The appearance of twenty million citizens overnight did not mean that there arose from the earth active citizens, committed at every national level to participation in public affairs. In 1789, in order to possess a theoretical right to equality, it was enough to have been 'born in France'; but for the militants of primary or sectional assemblies, everything still remained to be organized. Now let us consider the groups of Greeks two hundred or five hundred strong, such as those who, in the eighth and seventh centuries BC, were to establish themselves on sea-shores somewhere between Sicily and the Black Sea. Their potential 'citizenship' began with the tracing of a circle, called an *agora* (or assembly), or possibly with a drawing of lots for plots of land, either before their departure or aboard the ship itself. Each man, with his own set of weapons, seems already to have possessed an equal right to take part in debates and in sacrifices of foodstuffs made by the group as a whole. To participate and take part with an equal share in anything that belonged to whatever was 'in common' or concerned the city (*polis*) constituted the pulsing heart of this early type of citizenship centred on a fixed space reserved for assemblies, public debates, battles of words concerning the common affairs of an as yet barely established group. It is in these new places of equality and possibly 'of politics' that we can best observe the elements that continue to produce 'citizenship' centred upon 'common affairs'. It was not enough to be a local and to live on one's own plot of land. A man also had to take a hand in the dispensing of justice within another circle or a circle within a circle. How did 'citizens' wish to act as a group, and to what extent was it possible for them to do so? The nations of the past and their successive experiments in this domain are very useful when it comes to recognizing different types of citizenship and the criteria that make it possible to distinguish 'citizens' from foreigners passing through or in residence among them, and to establish a scale of gradations between those whose arrival could be accepted and those who could, to varying degrees, be integrated and furthermore 'naturalized'. For instance, should they or should they not be allowed access to public offices, to the highest posts as magistrates, or to other functions essential to the city or group? It has been noticed that, sooner or later, the assembly – the *universitas* or *community* – would come to expect an active citizen to manifest certain qualities before it ruled that he clearly did possess specific capabilities of a kind to guide the *Respublica* or its equivalent in a decisive fashion.

Those who are all the same and equal

A third point of entry or notion on which reflection proves rewarding is 'sameness-equality'. One hypothesis is that 'a will to assemble together in order to deliberate upon common affairs' presupposes that everyone recognizes all the others in this circle to be the same and somehow equal. The first analogy that springs to mind does not create a sameness great enough to envisage the possibility of 'a common interest'. Jean-Jacques Rousseau thought that the citizenship of the ancients was inspired by a common sensitivity born of the familiarity and compassion that existed among members of a very small homeland. He thought that in those times, a general will sprang up and flowed spontaneously. But the existence of similar sentiments and opinions is surely not the only conceivable basis for a community. The Cossacks shared a common desire to be 'free men' in the midst of princes and serfs, and all called one another 'brother'. Their common father was a leader whom they chose for themselves every year at the assembly of the 'brothers' who, through the practices of equality that they observed, were all 'the same' and 'equal'. From the start, the Cossacks were all 'free men' just as the participants in the first commune of eleventh-century Pisa were, for the most part, 'free' seamen who all shared the same struggle at sea. In other groups, all the members were Buddhist monks or secular canons.

In some societies, that sameness and equality was proclaimed explicitly, once a certain level of 'the will to assemble' was reached. For example, in ancient Greece, in the tiny cities of the archaic period, each man held equal rights and shared equally in the privileges of 'citizenship'. Such sameness presupposes that the distinctive features that, at a different level, distinguished men of different social status and with varying links of kinship would be set aside. Mutual recognition of forms of sameness may contribute to the creation of the idea of a community or city; and practices of equality, for their part, have a constant force. First there is an arithmetical equality in the distribution of land, of booty, or of food, all of which is shared out in equal portions allocated by the drawing of lots. Geometric equality soon follows, in a variety of formulations. And once, by one means or another, equality is discovered, it can become a war-cry, as it did at the end of the sixth century BC in Athens. The slogan was the word *isonomia*, 'having equal shares'. Equal shares of what? Of everything, of course – not that this always meant the cancellation of debts and a redistribution of land, as often happened in times of civil war. The Bostonians whom Tocqueville encountered in 1831 were content to enjoy equality in rights, but that was equality before God, who looked on from a considerable distance. Equality is something that needs to be made explicit, discussed in public and, in the usual way of things, fought for at every stage and at every assembly level. A theoretical equality can certainly bring to light the virtues of majority decisions in an assembly. However, strict equality geared to the domain of warrior practices can perfectly well accommodate the absence of one man, one vote for warriors who are all deemed to be the same.

Other points to follow up lie in wait, first and foremost the double issue of what is public and what is private. How can a public space be constructed and how does this affect the private space that is gradually discovered on the line separating one 'citizen' from another: citizens who are all the same and are concerned with equality, but who are individuals who are beginning – but how? – to stand out as being different on account of both certain individual traits and also individual interests? And then, of course, there is the difficult question of different types of men, or at least of those who seem at first glance to be more likely than others to glimpse the possibilities of a place for politics or in which to elaborate an egalitarian space: men such as warriors, monks, or merchants, to pick out only the most obvious.

This seems a good point at which to return to a series of lines of thought linked with 'the will to assemble', as found in the societies that we have studied. Here and there, they may perhaps awaken the curiosity of anyone venturing out to take the air beyond their own doorsteps.[6]

Everyone has the right to join an assembly[7]

South Africa's 1996 Bill of Rights was one of the new republic's triumphs: everyone now had a right to attend a meeting. There could be no better inauguration for a comparative approach than the courageous and contemporary experiment of a country that has for so long been dominated by apartheid. That ideology was designed at all costs to thwart the will-to-assemble-with-others of even two individuals, deemed obviously to be accomplices in a debate that was bound to be seditious.

Philippe-Joseph Salazar, a professor of 'parliamentary rhetoric', has revealed that the right to assemble because individuals wish to do so is neither something to take for granted nor necessarily a hard-won right. Common sense boggles in amazement. And that is a good sign.

Circles or semi-circles?[8]

Along with individuals who wish to assemble, a space is an essential component of practices involving speech on the subject of common affairs. Gathering in an assembly necessarily entails laying claim to some territory, spatially marking out the physical presence of people who wish to speak, listen, respond and argue and, in all probability, come to decisions. In fact, assembly places appear to be particularly prime choices when it comes to the architecture of a completely new kind of space: one in which a group chooses to make public an exchange of words that will forge the public discourse of a whole community.

Out of the regulated circulation of public speech between individuals who recognize one another to be equal, a kind of group self-consciousness emerges, or even the idea of a sovereignty for the people that operates through its assembly of representatives. Ever since 1789, the space marked out for members of the French Constituent Assembly has been a prime field of experimentation. Are some shapes bad for halls of assembly and others good? Now that architecture is concerned to promote civic virtues along with moral ones, the question is one that is much debated. So is a circle or a semi-circle better suited to symbolize equality, more in harmony with the idea of the people's sovereignty, better designed to promote the expression of a general will in all its heartfelt force? Drama, spectacle and politics are interrelated here, for politics need to be both shown and felt.

Places of equality[9]

Here are three examples from three different territories: the meeting places of Buddhist monks in medieval Japan, secular (that is to say, non-monastic) canons in France in the late Middle Ages, and initiates to the Senoufo societies of today's Ivory Coast. In Japan, the context is that of a break with the established order: a desire for justice administered by 'fair' individuals in a 'Council of State' independent of governmental institutions. Even as this happened, communities of monks were proclaiming their autonomy: they committed themselves to take into account all that concerned each and every one of them; they then sealed their commitment to one another with an oath acknowledging the authority of the gods present at the assembly. These monastic communities were economically powerful and could implement their decisions even in the face of the imperial court. In their assemblies, the rule of unanimity prevailed even though they observed the principle of one man, one vote. For the secular canons, the outlook was different. Theirs was an attempt to secure temporal power in the face of a Church characterized by hierarchical authority within a society of a royal nature that favoured a Gallican clergy. Can 'the practices of direct democracy' really have been a factor in the landscape of the medieval West? That same question should likewise be raised by the Italian communes. At a very early date there were certainly egalitarian assemblies that deliberated upon the clergy's communal affairs, and there were some clergy who endeavoured to reduce the inequalities among them. The idea of a *universitas* made its appearance, accompanied by its own particular symbolism: a seal, archives and a fixed meeting place. The canons' assembly favoured majority decisions based on written votes. In those two different medieval societies that knew nothing of each other, there were similar places of equality that were encouraging autonomous debates and decisions on the score of their own communal affairs. What is the significance of that? And how did they relate to other distinguishable places: merchant cities, village communities, the barracks of warrior-monks? What type of individual or even 'citizen' did this egalitarian impulse produce?

Among the Senoufo of the Ivory Coast, one attentive and patient ethnologist has discovered a kind of initiatory 'republic' the practices of which are designed to restore the primacy of equality on a daily basis. In a ritualized space in the shape of a semi-circle, the assembly devotes itself exclusively to a discussion of 'the affairs of the forest', that is to say, whatever is of common concern to the initiates of 'the Mother', in a society where every male individual is expected to undergo such initiation. At the centre of the forest assembly one place is left vacant, that of the 'Old Woman', the Mother of an incestuous lineage of children, but here she is a mother who, although without a mask through which to speak, is a figure who represents the central sovereignty of speech, an aspect of the Old Woman that is different from and additional to her involvement in initiation.

Beyond the forest and its place of equality, there is another assembly, one that manages the affairs of the village: it comprises a council and a group of chiefs and a whole band of hangers-on with all their inequalities and conflicting interests. This village council is made up of all the Senoufo adults who, each in turn, have been initiated in their forest. Is this an example of the cohabitation of just two out of many parallel systems and, if so, what is the nature of those others that may well exist on the continent of Africa, which is clearly so very rich in assemblies?

Warriors: Cossacks, Greeks and Circassians[10]

Now let us consider the warrior as a type of man, the warrior himself rather than warfare, which falls outside the scope encompassed by the beginnings of 'a will to assemble' in Cossack territory, the Greek cities, and nineteenth-century Circassia. Whereas the Greeks have been taken seriously for all too long, the Cossacks tend to be derided. Wrongly, for in this experimental enquiry, they certainly occupy an essential place.

This egalitarian circle of individuals who declare themselves to be 'free men' fascinates all those who wonder how and why it was that certain men in the vast emptiness of the Steppes rejected the power of masters and the despotism of a Muscovite Tsar and came to think of tracing out a circle that would give its name to their assembly. There would be a circle of 'equal brothers' that operated at every level of the organization of a society radically opposed to all forms of authoritarian power. Each year the most important of these assemblies chose the society's magistrates, war leaders, judges and secretaries, retaining the right to dismiss any of them at the demand of the most vociferous majority. This was a society of warriors that practised an egalitarian distribution of wealth, that is to say, land, income and booty, by the drawing of lots.

Might not such an egalitarian circle be invented several times over? Might the 'free men' among the early Zaporogues have observed Turko-Mongol communities? Were the Achaean warriors gathered in a circle on the Trojan sands heirs to an earlier tradition when they began to divide up their booty and share out portions of sacrificial meat in an egalitarian manner based on the drawing of lots? From the Bronze Age men of the *Iliad* down to the men of Sparta who declared themselves 'all similars', there emerges some kind of sovereignty that is held by an assembly committed to egalitarianism. So strong was this tendency that when, in the seventh century BC, disagreement arose among the 'leaders', the council doubtless included everyone gathered there and victory accordingly fell to the majority of the assembled people. A count of votes established the power, the *kratos*, of the people or *demos*. This was the first time that the term 'democracy', a form of people's sovereignty, appeared in the language of those natives. 'Who wishes to speak?' the herald would ask in the assembly gathered to deliberate upon war and all the military operations of each of those tiny cities. We know that the right to speak was inseparable from the ability to bear arms and fight alongside the rest of the citizens in the name initially of their 'common affairs' and, soon thereafter, of their little country.

A campaigning army could behave as a nomadic assembly that could rival the one that had remained 'in town', unless – that is – as in Sparta, the soldier-citizens had, before leaving, delegated the power of decision to those who remained at home, that is to say, in the case of Sparta, the Ephors and the council.

Beyond the land of the Cossacks, on the occasion of a radical clash with imperialist Russia in the nineteenth century, in the space of a few decades the Black Sea Circassian society invented a new kind of organization based upon a 'great constituent assembly'. This fleeting revolution began with a vast exodus of peasants, who moved away, liberating themselves from their rulers. New forms of social relations became necessary. Instead of gathering together the groups of lineages whose members were scattered far and wide throughout the Circassian territory, wise elders decided to proceed to a new kind of division that divided the society within the territory into 'groups of one hundred houses, these then being further divided into groups of ten'. A chequered pattern of centuries and decuries mobilized these warrior-peasants under a unified command that stemmed from the authority of the great Circassian assembly composed of the representatives sent by each group of one hundred houses.

Inventing the universitas[11]

Between the eleventh and twelfth centuries, Italian communes sprouted like mushrooms after the rain, each one a local experiment within a new public space. In general, the first thing that happened was that a collective group or *universitas* took shape, laying claim to an autonomy that aimed for self-government and the institution of an authority that was both secular and temporal. For this communal movement surfaced from deep in the midst of a society subject to the omnipresent authority of the Christian Church and also to that of the Germanic Holy Roman Empire. Gatherings before cathedrals when courts of justice were set up cannot be confused with the deliberate, planned assembly of seamen-citizens that took place in Pisa in 1080. This decreed itself to be a *communitas* and assumed the right to organize and finance armed expeditions of its fleet. Elsewhere, too, the conquest of a civic space proceeded step by step, involving a whole series of microscopic regulatory measures: the alignment of houses, the positioning of streets, the management of town gates and the design of public places.

Consuls, assemblies and councils continued to be features characteristic of the history of communal practices. (It is perhaps worth noting, in passing, that many such communes are still awaiting a historian.) One primary aspect of this world of communes is the role played by notaries and jurists. Dispensing justice and declaring the rights of citizens are activities that go hand in hand with the work of the notaries who consign the debates to written records, thereby formulating practices many of which are without precedent. Another feature that played an important role in the creation of communal assemblies was the taking of an oath of solidarity and loyalty to the collective decisions that committed the community to action. In some cases, such an oath would be individual, in others collective. It indicated that the will-to-assemble counted for more than the mere traditional gatherings of the past. What forms of citizenship do we find developing in these emerging 'city-republics'? What was the basis of the sameness of those who agreed to decide together upon affairs that affected the *communitas* as a whole? An assembly that might be called a 'parliament' often takes the form of a *populus*, meaning all those capable of bearing arms on both land and sea and who must have possessed sufficient means to pay for arms and, in some cases, a horse. Here and there we find instances of a *populus* that splits away from the *milites* who fight on horseback while the rest continue to do so on foot. Councils restricted to between three and five hundred members set about preparing the agenda and discussing the major issues before submitting them to a general assembly that might be composed of between five and six thousand members. Some modes of election involved the drawing of lots, others did not. There were rules relating to majority votes, the definition of a quorum and the roles of experts and social leaders. All such procedures varied from one commune to another and produced types of 'politics' that inevitably varied from one place to another.

Holding an assembly[12]

In Syria in 1800 BC, gatherings were very common. They would take place at the town gates, at the centre of the kingdom, in regional councils and even in certain cities. In most cases, these were gatherings instigated by some royal figure or a leader with authority delegated by the current king. 'The right to assemble' was not necessarily held by every individual; moreover, once an assembly was in place, the right to speech was carefully controlled. Figures of Thersites' ilk were promptly ejected. Neither Bedouin clans nor subjects bearing arms appear to have claimed special rights on the basis of their status as warriors. Certain merchant towns positioned at the crossroads of several kingdoms produced city assemblies and councils that welcomed a taste of autonomy to settle various communal affairs.

Deliberations were courteous. Speech was left to the most important figures, usually the elders and social leaders, who were acutely aware of the benefits of consensus and unanimity. Such seems to have been the general practice in both the Near and the Middle East. An assembly was 'a forum in which honour, esteem, respect and modesty prevailed'. Being present at a common assembly was probably a delight, like being together as a family. In the South Pacific too, there were great assemblies and even fine, rich houses in which to enjoy them at one's leisure. The topography of such houses can only be deciphered with a perfect understanding of the kinship groups that structure the space, both the 'private' part and the 'public' domain that was reserved for discussions and debates on the subject of communal affairs. Austronesians could not manage without the grandeur of their kings. They cultivated hereditary privileges and emblems that enhanced the prestige of much coveted responsibilities. Banquets and debates alternated in a very civilized manner. No assembly passed without copious gift-giving; and the pooling of goods and food was followed by a distribution that had no specific reason to be egalitarian. First those present ate and drank; then they held a debate. About what? The clearing of land, collective fishing, the upkeep of coconut groves. Publicity for a whole series of acts and decisions was assured by the use of the formula 'The assembly house declares . . .'. And what happens today?

The House of Commons and the members of the French Constituent Assembly[13]

The scene changes. In France, the theatre of representation is the Constituent Assembly; in England, the House of Commons. There is also a temporal disparity here. When the French Revolution of 1789 began, English practices had long been simmering, for in the fourteenth and fifteenth centuries the London Parliament had been extremely active. The French Constituent Assembly inaugurated a new space for speech, as the sovereignty of the people required a new public space: there were disputes over the advantages of a circle and those of a semi-circle. In 1792, new practices were introduced, at the instigation of both Marseilles and Paris. It was no longer just a matter of every individual's right to assemble; now, every citizen was claiming the right to 'make the law speak'. It was time to move beyond the restricted circle of the Assembly and its representatives. Room had to be made for the missionaries of patriotism whose tramping feet were beginning to furrow the roads of Provence. The people exercised their sovereignty as they marched. Practices that developed as they marched together produced citizens convinced that assemblies at a primary level should be open to all those 'of French nationality', provided, of course, they carried a section-card. Spokesmen arose to voice the passions that expressed the 'moral needs' of the sovereign people. The cold Assembly legislators were invited to manifest due sensitivity; they must be receptive to the emotions of the people. On a spontaneous impulse, there would be declarations of the sacred nature of this 'surge of emergent people's power'. New assembly practices such as these clearly called for a change of scene. In Marseilles, where people knew how to gauge the force of this deliberative movement, a central committee took on the task of producing a 'general consensus'. It would be interesting to know how the Soviets proceeded at the time of the early Bolsheviks and Comrade Lenin. However, the enquiry pursued by historians and ethnologists ever since 1992 has unfortunately not provided us with any such documentation.

In the aftermath of 1789, in order to set up dialogue between the 1,200 elected members of the Constituent Assembly, who were determined 'to imitate nobody', it was first necessary to establish control over the agenda, in order to pass new laws and take the necessary financial decisions. How could a chance to speak be won? How could the discussion be focused in such a way as to keep it egalitarian yet have it proceed by way of a series of orderly motions? Soon, a number of virtually permanent committees were created, the operations of which were essential for the new 'twenty million' citizens. Fortunately, many of these mechanisms had already been tried and tested by the House of Commons of Great Britain, although significant differences remained: for example, the members of the Constituent Assembly elected themselves a new president every two weeks. There was no question of electing a Speaker for the entire duration of a Parliament, as in England where this person may remain in place for seven years. In this connection, it would be useful to set up a comparison relating to different kinds of beginnings, particularly the beginnings of London's House of Commons, whose practices involve a whole parliamentary rhetoric the effects of which, after a succession of adjustments, are likely still to mark the European assemblies of Strasbourg today and in the future.

A 'place for politics'[14]

In the mountains of southern Ethiopia, one ethnologist has rediscovered a society that still believes today that power should lie in the assembly. In Addis Ababa, these people are regarded as savages.

In Paris, they are not considered African. But the fact remains that these non-African savages have invented a society in which hierarchy is constantly challenged. Whoever takes the trouble to visit them or, better still, revisit them, will notice that the stone seats arranged in a circular sweep are set on the highest possible site for an assembly. There is no centralized power, only assemblies in which social status and kinship links count for nothing. Better still, among the Ochollo people, it is the sacrificers, whose function is hereditary, who organize all ritual activities, including all ceremonial as – in this respect at least – is customary in many African societies. The sacrificers are integrated into the circular assembly but take no active part in its debates. Because they are so powerful, they are required to remain silent and may only intervene when it comes to establishing a final consensus. In contrast, however, room is made for new actors considered to be 'dignitaries', good orators and agents of the forum, who speak for common interests. When it comes to sacrifices – for these constitute a part of public affairs just as do irrigation projects and warfare – it is the assembly that, in sovereign fashion, decides on the number of victims as well as who should perform the ritual.

How to compare and why[15]

In this collaborative comparativism it is not, nor will ever be, a matter of juxtaposing a dash of Japan that in some inexplicable way sums up the whole of Japan, a flavour of the Circassians to represent the entire mass of the Caucasus all in one go and, just to add a touch of colour, two or three Italian communes, so as to justify writing, in conclusion to a volume of the 'Comparative Studies' ilk, 'This is how people assembled together in Italy and invented politics there, while in Japan . . .' That would be to travel far and wide as dupes, only to resume the society game played by Hellenists for whom nothing is more exciting than discovering whether *our* Athenians really experienced 'Democracy', real democracy, or – a more refined variant of the same theme – whether it was Solon or Cleisthenes who should be honoured forever for having invented politics (*le politique* in French: but why a singular noun? Most peculiar . . .).

The eye of a comparativist discerns practices associated with the act of assembling that might very well not have been adopted or that might have engendered other kinds of equality. He/she also discerns practices that may die out: alongside tentative advances and lightning manifestations, some achievements that have won acceptance, possibly over several centuries, seem to have been made possible only thanks to the evanescence of other experiments, now forgotten, never mentioned, gone forever. History, the kind taught in schools and universities, offers us the fascinating study of *our* Greeks, who belong to *us* (or is it the other way around?) without even considering more modern peoples and aspects of their lives. But anthropology meanwhile wakes up comparative every morning, free to flit from culture to culture, gathering its honey wherever the will to assemble has sprouted and bloomed. With its taste for dissonance, anthropology invites us to focus upon societies that present contrasts that may seem either excessive or mysterious, depending on the view of the observer who comes upon them. Unchecked by frontiers in space or time, anthropology collects them all, separates them out and goes on to discover others, elsewhere. But why? (For that question resurfaces like an uncheckable weed as soon as scholarship becomes concerned about this discipline and its future.) In the first place, because setting a number of experiments in perspective usually reveals areas of intelligibility the value and flexibility of which are recognized by both historians of politics and even philosophers, in their own domains of study; secondly, because a collection of beginnings, observed in the concrete process of their evolution, may make it possible to analyse, as if under a microscope, the components of neighbouring configurations, each of which, with its own particular differential features, may help an attentive comparativist to spot the deviation from the norm that distinguishes among a whole series of possibilities the particular formula of one micro-configuration of politics.

Afterword

As can be seen, doing anthropology with the Greeks is not the easiest thing in the world, but nor is it the least stimulating. Relations between the Greeks and us tend to be conflictual, and so they should be, given that general feeling, *our* general feeling favours the view that our history begins with the Greeks and, as everyone intuitively knows, the Greeks are not 'like others'.

To be sure, ancient Greece is a part of humanity's past. It belongs to a whole group of ancient societies, such as Mesopotamia, China, Egypt and Vedic India. But in Europe each of us senses that Greece cannot be confused with Sumer and its tablets, nor with Egypt and its pyramids. Thanks to an ages-old tradition, passed down by successive humanist movements, we have the feeling that we are closer to the Greeks of those beginnings that occurred between the *Odyssey* and Parmenides or between Homer and the Parthenon.

We sense both proximity and distance. For more than a century we historians and anthropologists of good faith have been making the most of both. As I have remarked before, the founders of anthropology did not set ancient Greece apart from cultures described as primitive or without civilization; and certain historians and Hellenists without history have gone along with them on a series of expeditions in unknown lands.

Hellenists among anthropologists? What exactly is going on? It is worth pausing to consider. In the contemporary world, Hellenists start from the same position as historians, who are always wondering, in a circumspect fashion, what gives one the right to compare and whether or not ethnology is useful to ancient history or an understanding of Greek literature. Is that too much of a caricature? I think not and would like to make a couple of observations for the benefit of those disinclined to agree with me.

In the minds of even intelligent and cultivated Hellenists, the word 'anthropology' often evokes the idea of a science devoted to the measurement of skulls and the classification of various 'races' according to their physical characteristics: a science of capital importance, as Charles Seignobos, an honest-to-God historian of the French nation, used to say, pointing out that such a science would make it possible to establish who were the ancestors of the population of France. Of course, nowadays, other Greek and Latin specialists claim to have it on the best authority that anthropology, the kind taught in universities, is a discipline reserved for societies threatened with extinction or little communities left on the shelf in history – the kind of history that makes out everything to be historical right from the start.

My second observation is more idiosyncratic. One of the peculiarities of the way that Hellenists and their faithful followers conceive of the history of Greece lies in their sincere and stubborn refusal to find it remarkable or to be astonished at the cultural inventions of the ancient Greeks and Romans in comparison to other societies. That is just a way to continue as heirs to the 'Greek miracle' of our textbooks and not to have to think any more about it. It is as if that is established by affidavit: the Greeks, *our* Greeks are not like others. No need to discuss the matter further, it's part of academic routine.

What comes next is more interesting and it stems from that double sense of proximity and distance that was so vividly described many years ago by the author of *La Cité antique*, Fustel de Coulange. We ourselves are not Greeks, we share neither their conception of liberty nor their vision of politics, and yet they are our closest neighbours. Very well. But does that mean that we should dismiss the idea of comparativism and experimentation with societies both distant from and close to us?

Let us imagine a scenario that might bear the title 'A Return to the Greeks' (but that has nothing to do with science fiction). Historians and Hellenists fired with enthusiasm decide to set off to discover who 'Greek man' really was. Sickened by the platitude of the idea of some kind of eternal Greece, they determine to track down the marvellous strangeness of the Greeks, the factor that makes them, of all archaic societies, so particularly fascinating. They endeavour to get as close as possible to their forms of sensibility and thought, to track down their society's most secret ways of thinking and all the notions and categories that they employ to speak of time, the will and the person. They conduct themselves as genuine ethnographers working on a terrain that they need to clear, listening to the language spoken by their hosts and striving to catch its every nuance and even their most intimate reactions. They would be delighted to discover that the Greeks come first in everything, that it is they who invented philosophy and the city, money and geometry, and they who testify brilliantly to the moment in the history of humanity when human beings underwent a very sudden and very radical change. The otherness of these new Greeks seems to their investigators so desirable that they allow themselves to speak of them using only the Greeks' own words and own conceptual language. No doubt such historians would find themselves at last close to reaching the Greeks in all their authenticity and revealed specificity. They might even congratulate themselves upon having discovered an approach that could harmoniously combine the recommended degree of empathy with the long-distance view that was always *de rigueur*.

The illusion would be perfect and an anthropology of ancient Greece would be born. However, upon closer scrutiny might it not turn out that these fictional historians and Hellenists, who had set off with such high hopes and winged heels, at the end of their journey found themselves in the company of the most sedentary of their colleagues, surrounded on all sides by those who profess to love the Greeks merely through atavism. Would they not have been labouring, albeit under the sign of authenticity, to produce a history of *our* Greeks, that is to say the Greeks for us, even if they claimed them to be the subjects of an 'exotic' anthropology that some, forging a neologism, would boldly claim to be 'historical anthropology'? Of course, it might involve a stimulating approach to Greek categories or even to Greek thought as a whole. However, as a result of being committed by its attachment to such a remarkable specificity and otherness, that approach would be bound to trap those who adopted it within the exclusive circle confined to our closest and best neighbours, the Greeks, who are, as ever, *our* Greeks.

We ought to be engaging in anthropology *with* the Greeks, rather than in an anthropology-cum-history of the Greeks. Anthropology was born comparative at about the same time as history became national and looked to chronological time to select its objects and determine their meaning. Anthropology that sets out to be comparative must necessarily be carried out by ethnologists doing field-work in collaboration with historians of specific territories. Historians and ethnologists need to work together. Reflecting comparatively at every turn upon partly local, partly general questions makes it necessary to analyse certain microconfigurations and specific constellations of practices, but to do so with a view to comparing them, picking out their components and distinguishing the various ways in which they are put together. In short, in order to *construct* comparabilities that are fruitful, one needs to 'experiment'.

This involves moving around in the space and time of a variety of cultures and societies, going to the furthest reaches of inhabited lands and delving into their pasts right to the limit of the unknown. To embark upon setting exotic and distant societies in perspective alongside the ancient configurations of 'our' own societies is to enter a laboratory of *completed experiments* of an apparently limitless richness. Anthropologists and historians readily agree that a general question – such as those singled out in this book – may allow a historian to escape from confinement within a particular period and an anthropologist to leap over the bounds of his/her particular territory. The historian-anthropologist will, for his/her part, use the past as a store of experiments upon which to reflect; meanwhile the anthropologist-historian will set about exploring the repository of cultural experiments that have been and continue to be made throughout the world.

By setting their sights on the variabilities of cultures, those who practise this kind of comparative anthropology magnetized by dissonances will reveal the paucity of corporatisms carefully pigeon-holed into 'disciplines'. They will draw attention to the stupidity of incomparability and of all that claims or seems to be 'incomparable', whether it be 'Greece' or 'the Nation' or, as often happens, both at once.

Fear not: we do not need to uncover the laws of the mind in our increasingly multicultural societies, in order to carry out exercises that will enable us to understand that which seems strange or distant even in what is most familiar.

Notes and References

Chapter 1   Doing Anthropology *with* the Greeks

1 Didier Eribon, Claude Lévi-Strauss, *De près et de loin*, Paris, 1984, p. 84.

2 See Jean Pépin, *Idées grecques sur l'homme et sur dieu*, Paris, 1971, pp. 1–51. On 'theologia' or the meaning of *theologos*, see Victor Goldschmidt, *Questions platoniciennes*, Paris, 1970, pp. 141–72; also, for a different approach, Richard Bodeü, *Aristote et la théologie des vivants immortels*, Paris, 1992, pp. 301–35 ('Théologie et façons de parler').

3 Aristotle, *Nicomachean Ethics*, IV, 8, 1125 a 5.

4 References in Jean Copans, *Introduction à l'ethnologie et à l'anthropologie*, Paris, 1996. Others, many of them extremely suggestive, in the *Dictionnaire de l'ethnologie et de l'anthropologie*, Michel Izard and Pierre Bonte (eds), Paris, 1991.

5 E.g. Henri Pinard de la Boullaye, *L'Etude comparée des religions*, Paris, 1925, pp. 151–75; Philippe Borgeaud, *Aux origines de l'histoire des religions*, Paris, 2004.

6 Let me refer the reader to *Comparer l'incomparable*, Paris, 2000, pp. 17–39 ('Si d'aventure un anthropologue rencontre un historien', still relevant).

7 See Robert Ackerman, *J. G. Frazer: his Life and Work*, Cambridge, 1987.

8 See Marcel Detienne, *Comment être autochtone*, Paris, 2003, pp. 123–49 ('Grandeur du français raciné').

9 Emile Durkheim, *Textes*, V. Karady (ed.), vol. III, Paris, 1975, pp. 160–3; 178–224.

10 See Emile Durkheim, *Les Règles de la méthode sociologique*, Paris, 1937 (reprinted 2002), pp. 124–38.

11 On the complicities, conflicts and distances between 'Hellenists' and
    anthropology, see an earlier essay of mine: 'Rentrer au village: un tro-
    pisme de l'hellénisme?', *L'Homme*, 157, 2001, pp. 137–50 (English
    version: 'Back to the village: a tropism of Hellenists?' *History of
    Religions*, 2001, pp. 99–113).
12 See Marcel Detienne, 'Avec ou sans écriture?', the Introduction to
    the file entitled 'Les écritures', *Sciences de l'Homme et de la Société*,
    Department letter, no. 60, December 2000, pp. 3–6. For reflections
    on 'historical discourse/ethnological discourse', see Michèle Duchet,
    Le Partage des savoirs, Paris, 1985. On 'anthropology and history'
    (both yesterday and today, in France), see in particular Gérard
    Lenclud, in *Ethnologies en miroir*, I. Chiva and V. Jeggle (eds), Paris,
    1987, pp. 35–65.
13 Claude Lévi-Strauss, 'Religions comparées des peuples sans écriture'
    in *Problèmes et méthodes d'histoire des religions*, Paris, 1968, pp. 1–4.
14 Lewis Morgan, *Ancient Society*, New York, 1877.
15 Ernest Lavisse, *Instructions de 1890*, cited by François Furet, *L'Atelier
    de l'histoire*, Paris, 1982, pp. 119–20.
16 As continues, frequently, to be noted, most recently by Jacqueline de
    Romilly and Jean-Pierre Vernant, *Pour l'amour du grec*, Paris, 2000,
    pp. 5–28.
17 Marcel Detienne, 'Les Grecs ne sont pas comme les autres', *Critique*,
    no. 332, 1975, pp. 3–24; *Dionysos mis à mort*, Paris, coll. 'Tel', 1999
    (*Dionysos Slain*, translated by M. Muellner and L. Muellner,
    Baltimore, 1975).
18 See Marcel Detienne, 'La mythologie scandaleuse', *Traverses*, 12,
    1978, pp. 3–19.
19 See, for example, despite his philosophical understanding of 'multi-
    culturalism', Charles Taylor, *Multiculturalism and 'the Politics of
    Recognition'*, Princeton, 1992.
20 This is the subject of ch. 2.
21 This is the subject of ch. 3.
22 This is the subject of ch. 4.
23 See ch. 6.
24 For an initial approach, see *Comparer l'incomparable*, op.cit.,
    pp. 61–80 ('Mettre en perspective les régimes d'historicité').
25 Op.cit., pp. 113–19.
26 After 'Construire des comparables' (in *Comparer l'incomparable*,
    op. cit., pp. 41–59), I returned to the subject in 'L'Art de construire
    des comparables. Entre historiens et anthropologues', *Critique inter-
    nationale*, no. 14, 2002, pp. 68–78, in the hope of attracting the

attention of a few anthropologists, if not certain historians. See also, for Anglo-Saxon readers, 'Murderous Identity. Anthropology, History and the Art of Constructing Comparables', *Common Knowledge*, 2002, 8(1), pp. 178–87.

27 The kind of comparativism that I am championing is thus different from that practised by Georges Dumézil and Claude Lévi-Strauss. Both those authors maintain that nothing should be compared that cannot be related to a common area – for the former, the domain of Indo-European languages, for the latter the historical and geographical unity of America.

28 'L'exercice de la comparaison, au plus proche, à distance'. A colloquium organized by Lucette Valensi at the EHESS, and published under her editorship in *Annales HSS*, 2002, 57(1), pp. 27–144.

29 I am here inspired by an example chosen by Clifford Geertz, *Local Knowledge. Further Essays in Interpretive Anthropology*, New York, p. 64–70, the more easily given that on this side of the Atlantic, 'the person' was a favourite subject for a comparative approach in the 1960s, a fact that American anthropologists continue to ignore. See e.g. Ignace Meyerson (ed.), *Problèmes de la personne*, Paris, 1973.

30 Clifford Geertz, *Local Knowledge* . . ., op. cit., pp. 64–70.

31 This is the clearest example. I used it in *Comparer l'incomparable*, op. cit., pp. 44–56, having previously used it in Marcel Detienne (ed.), *Tracés de fondation*, Paris-Louvain, 1990, pp. 1–16.

Chapter 2   From Myth to Mythology

1 On all the material contained in 'From Myth to Mythology', see the texts and the more fully developed comments in my *L'Invention de la mythologie*, Paris (1981), coll. 'Tel', 1992, 242 pp. A slightly different version of this chapter has appeared in English ('From Myth to Mythology') in *The Writing of Orpheus. Greek Myth in Cultural Context*, translated by Janet Lloyd, Baltimore and London, 2003, p. 199 (a new version of *L'Ecriture d'Orphée*, Paris, coll. 'L'Infini', 1989).

Here, arranged in alphabetical order, is a selective bibliography that should be useful for further study of similar problems and questions:

Blaise, Fabienne, 'Les formes narratives et littéraires des mythes grecs', *Quaderni Urbinati di Cultura Classica*, 42, 3, 1992, pp. 131–7

Borgeaud, Philippe, *Recherches sur le dieu Pan*, Institut suisse de Rome, 1979 (*The Cult of Paris in Ancient Greece*, translated by Kathleen Atlass and James Redfield, Chicago, 1988)
— *Aux origines de l'histoire des religions*, Paris, 2004
Brisson, Luc, *Platon. Les mots et les mythes* (1982), Paris, 1994 (2nd edn)
Burkert, Walter, *Homo Necans: Interpretation altgriechischer Opferriten und Mythen*, Berlin-New York, 1972 (*Homo Necans*, translated by Peter Bing, Berkeley, 1983)
— *Structure and History in Greek Mythology and Ritual*, Berkeley-Los Angeles, 1979
Buxton, Richard (ed.), *From Myth to Reason? Studies in the Development of Greek Thought*, Oxford, 1999
Calame, Claude (ed.), *Métamorphoses du mythe en Grèce antique*, Geneva, 1988
— *Le Récit en Grèce ancienne. Enonciations et représentations de poètes*, Paris, 1986
Detienne, Marcel and Jean-Pierre Vernant, *Cunning Intelligence in Greek Culture and Society*, translated by Janet Lloyd, Hassocks (Sussex) and New Jersey, 1978
Detienne, Marcel, *The Gardens of Adonis. Spices in Greek Mythology* translated by Janet Lloyd, Princeton, 1994
— *Dionysos Slain*, translated by M. Muellner and L. Muellner, Baltimore, 1975
— *L'Invention de la mythologie*, Paris (1981), coll. 'Tel', 1992 (*The Creation of Mythology*, translated by Margaret Cook, Chicago, 1986)
— *The Writing of Orpheus. Greek Myth in Cultural Context*, translated by Janet Lloyd, Baltimore-London, 2003
— *Apollon, le couteau à la main*, Paris, 1998
— (ed.) *Transcrire les mythologies. Tradition, écriture, historicité*, Paris, 1994
Edmunds, L. (ed.), *Approaches to Greek Myth*, Baltimore-London, 1990
Ellinger, Pierre, *La Légende nationale phocidienne. Artémis, les situations extrêmes et les récits de guerre d'anéantissement*, Athens-Paris, 1993
Gentili, Bruno and Paioni, Giuseppe (ed.), *Il mito greco*, Rome, 1977
Gernet, Louis, *Anthropologie de la Grèce antique*, Paris, 1968
Goody, Jack, *The Domestication of the Savage Mind*, Cambridge, 1977
Gordon, R. L. (ed.), *Myth, Religion and Society. Structuralist Essays by M. Detienne, L. Gernet, J.-P. Vernant and P. Vidal-Naquet*, Cambridge, 1982

Graf, Fritz, *Greek Mythology. An Introduction*(1987), translated by Thomas Marier, Baltimore-London, 1993

Greimas, Algirdas, *Des dieux et des hommes*, Paris, 1985

Jacob, Christian, 'Problèmes de lecture du mythe grec', *Le Conte* (Albi Colloquium), Toulouse, 1987, pp. 389–408

Lévi-Strauss, Claude, *Anthropologie structurale*, Paris, 1958 (*Structural Anthropology*, translated by Claire Jacobson and Brooke Grundfest Schoepf, Harmondsworth, 1997)

— *Anthropologie structurale*, 2, Paris, Plon, 1973 (*Structural Anthropology 2*, translated by Monique Layton, Harmondsworth, 1978)

— *Textes de et sur Claude Lévi-Strauss*, collected by R. Bellour and C. Clément, Paris, 1979

— 'De la fidélité au texte', *L'Homme*, CI, 1987, pp. 117–40

— *Mythologiques*, vol. I–IV, Paris, 1964–1971 (English translation, London, 1994)

— *Paroles données*, Paris, 1964–1971 (*Anthropology and Myth*, translated by Roy Willis, Oxford, 1987)

— *La Potière jalouse*, Paris, 1985 (*The Jealous Potter*, translated by Bénédicte Chorier, Chicago-London, 1988)

— *Histoire de Lynx*, Paris, 1990 (*The Story of Lynx*, translated by Catherine Tihanyi, Chicago, 1995)

Lincoln, Bruce, *Theorizing Myth, Narrative, Ideology and Scholarship*, Chicago, 1999

Nagy, Gregory, *The Best of the Achaeans: Concepts of the Hero in Archaic Greek Poetry*, Baltimore, 1979

— *Greek Mythology and Poetics*, Ithaca, 1990

— *Pindar's Homer: the Lyric Possession of an Epic Past*, Baltimore, 1990

— *Poetry as Performance. Homer and Beyond*, Cambridge, 1996

Schlesier, Renate (ed.), *Faszination des Mythos*, Basel and Frankfurt am Main, 1985

Smith, Pierre, 'La nature des mythes', *Diogène*, 82, 1973, pp. 91–108

— *Le Récit populaire au Rwanda*, Paris, 1975

Smyth-Florentin, Françoise, *Les Mythes illégitimes. Essai sur la 'terre promise'*, Geneva, 1994

Vernant, Jean-Pierre, *Myth and Thought among the Greeks*, (1965) London, 1983

— *Myth and Society in Ancient Greece*, (1974) translated by Janet Lloyd, New York, 1988

Veyne, Paul, *Les Grecs ont-ils cru à leurs mythes? Essai sur l'imagination constituante*, Paris, 1983 (*Did the Greeks Believe in Their*

Myths? An Essay on the Constitutive Imagination, translated by
Paula Wissing, Chicago, 1988)

Chapter 3   Transcribing Mythologies

1 Marcel Detienne, 'Repenser la mythologie', in Michel Izard
   and Pierre Smith (eds), *La Fonction symbolique*, Paris, 1979,
   pp. 71–82.
2 The formula is Claude Lévi-Strauss's, from *Anthropologie structurale*,
   Paris, 1958, p. 232 (*Structural Anthropology*, translated by Claire
   Jacobson and Brooke Grundfest Schoepf, Harmondsworth, 1997).
   'Reader' should be firmly underlined.
3 The idea of a collective enquiry emerged following that which
   resulted in *Tracés de fondation*, Bibliothèque de l'Ecole pratique des
   hautes études, Sciences religieuses, Paris-Louvain, 1990.
4 François Macé, 'La double écriture des traditions dans le Japon du
   VIIIe siècle. Fondation et refondation, histoire et recommence-
   ments', in Marcel Detienne (ed.), *Transcrire les mythologies*, Paris,
   1994, pp. 77–102; notes, pp. 254–5.
5 Alban Bensa, 'Vers Kanaky, tradition orale et idéologie nationaliste
   en Nouvelle-Calédonie', in Jocelyne Fernandez-Vest (ed.), *Kalevala
   et traditions orales du monde*, Paris, 1987, pp. 423–38.
6 See for example, Colette Beaune, *Naissance de la nation France*, Paris,
   1985, pp. 19–54; Bernard Guénée, *Politique et Histoire au Moyen
   Age*, Paris, 1987.
7 See A. Paul, *Le Judaïsme ancien et la Bible*, Paris, 1987.
8 Y. Yerushalmi, *Zakhor. Histoire juive et mémoire juive*, Paris, 1984.
9 As with Sumerian and Minoan: L. Godart, *Le Pouvoir de l'écrit. Au
   pays des premières écritures*, Paris, 1990.
10 I strongly recommend Mario Vegetti's study, 'Dans l'ombre de
   Thoth. Dynamique de l'écriture chez Platon', in Marcel Detienne
   (ed.), *Les Savoirs de l'écriture. En Grèce ancienne*, Lille, 1992 (1st edn,
   1988), pp. 387–419. It should provide food for thought for anyone
   inclined, out of habit and piety, to look no further than a few lines
   from the *Phaedrus*.
11 See the excellent chapter by Christian Jacob, 'L'ordre généalogique.
   Entre le mythe et l'histoire', in *Transcrire les mythologies . . .*, op. cit.,
   pp. 169–202; pp. 240–5.
12 See the rich enquiry entitled *La Création dans l'Orient ancien*, Paris,
   1988. I have explained this comparison in 'Fondare, creare, pensare

l'inizio tra la Grecia e Israele', in L. Preta (ed.), *La Narrazione delle origini*, Bari-Rome, 1991, pp. 109–16, and also in my remarks in 'Manières grecques de commencer', in *Transcrire les mythologies* . . ., op. cit., pp. 159–66; 235–6.

13 See for example, J. Gabriel, 'Die Kainitengenealogie', *Biblica*, 40, 1959, pp. 409–27; J. M. Miller, 'The descendants of Cain. Notes on *Genesis* 4', *Zeitschrift für die altestamentliche Wissenschaft*, 86, 1974, pp. 164–74. I am grateful to Sergio Ribichini who provided me with these references. But on this question, the most incisive work is J. Ellul, *Sans feu ni lieu. Signification biblique de la grande ville*, Paris, 1976.

14 See Gilbert Hamonic, 'L'Histoire, comme éclatée . . . deux ordres de conservation du passé en pays bugis-makassar (Célèbes-Sud, Indonésie)', in *Transcrire les mythologies* . . ., op. cit., pp. 114–28; pp. 255–6.

15 'Qu'est-ce que la tradition?' in *Transcrire les mythologies* . . ., op. cit., pp. 25–44; pp. 250–1; see also a reworked version, 'History and Tradition', in Marie Mauzé (ed.), *Present is Past*, Lanham, Md., 1997, pp. 43–64.

16 'Paroles durables, écritures perdues. Réflexions sur la pictographie cuna', in *Transcrire les mythologies* . . ., op. cit., pp. 45–73; pp. 228–32; pp. 251–4.

17 Hecataeus retains a strategic position (see *L'Invention de la mythologie*, Paris, 1992, pp. 134–5). For pertinent nuances and questions, see François Hartog, 'Ecritures, généalogies, archives, histoire en Grèce', in *Mélanges Pierre Lévêque*, Besançon, 1991, vol. V, pp. 181–3.

18 The project has been sketched in, in a chapter in Marcel Detienne, *Comparer l'incomparable*, Paris, 2000, pp. 61–80 ('Mettre en perspective les régimes d'historicité'), which is still relevant.

19 John Scheid, 'Le Temps de la cité et l'histoire des prêtres. Des origines religieuses de l'histoire romaine', in *Transcrire les mythologies* . . ., op. cit., pp. 149–58; pp. 237–8; p. 258.

20 Georges Dumézil, *La Religion romaine archaïque*, Paris, 1974 (1st edn, 1966), p. 118.

21 Claude Lévi-Strauss, *L'Origine des manières de table*, Paris, 1968, p. 355 (*The Origin of Table Manners*, translated by John and Doreen Weightman, London, 1978) which is based on the analysis by Salomon Reinach, 'Une prédiction accomplie', in *Cultes, Mythes et Religions*, III, 1908, pp. 302–10; and J. Hubaux, *Les Grands Mythes de Rome*, Paris, 1945, which was so innovative in its reading of the relations that the Romans established between a limited time-span and a *stable* place.

22 L. Vandermeersch, 'Vérité historique et langage de l'histoire en Chine', in A. Lichnerovicz and G. Gadoffre (eds), *La vérité est-elle scientifique?* Paris, 1989, p. 72. On 'History and Divination', a theme rich in comparativist perspectives, see Léon Vandermeersch, 'L'Imaginaire divinatoire dans l'histoire en Chine', in *Transcrire les mythologies* . . ., op. cit., pp. 103–13; pp. 234–5.
23 'Vérité historique . . .', op. cit., p. 72.
24 Ibid., pp. 73–5.
25 Marcel Detienne, 'L'Espace de la publicité: ses opérateurs intellectuels dans la cité', in Marcel Detienne (ed.), *les Savoirs de l'écriture. En Grèce ancienne*, Lille, 1992 (1988, 1st edn), pp. 67–70.
26 Claude Lévi-Strauss, *Paroles données*, Paris, 1984, pp. 150–7 ('Ordre et désordre dans la tradition orale') (*Anthropology and Myth*, translated by Roy Willis, Oxford, 1987).

Chapter 4   The Wide-Open Mouth of Truth

1 For instance, Jacqueline de Romilly, *Pourquoi la Grèce?*, Paris, 1992, p. 298.
2 In chronological order, *Homère, Hesiode et Pythagore, Poésie et philosophie dans le pythagorisme ancien*, Latomus collection, vol. LVII, Brussels, 1962; *De la pensée religieuse à la pensée philosophique. La notion de Daïmôn dans le pythagorisme ancien*, Bibliothèque de la faculté de philosophie et lettres de l'université de Liège, vol. CLXV, Paris, 1963; *Crise agraire et attitude religieuse chez Hésiode*, Latomus collection, vol. LXVIII, Brussels, 1963.
3 'La notion mythique d'*Alétheia*', *Revue des études grecques*, vol. LXXIII, 1960, pp. 27–35.
4 Michel Foucault, *L'Ordre du discours*, Paris, 1971, p. 17.
5 Hesiod, *Theogony*, 27–8.
6 Louis Gernet, 'Les origines de la philosophie', *Bulletin de l'Enseignement public du Maroc*, no. CLXXXIII, 1945, pp. 1–2.
7 Three of them: Ignace Meyerson, with his 'historical and comparative' psychology, which he claimed to be the only really Marxist psychology, as did his two most faithful disciples; Louis Gernet and Jean-Pierre Vernant, the latter perhaps rather reluctantly.
8 Paris, 1968, pp. 415–30.
9 Op. cit., p. 1.
10 In particular, in chap. XI: 'La structure des mythes', *Anthropologie structurale*, Paris, 1958, pp. 227–55 (*Structural Anthropology*,

translated by Claire Jacobson and Brooke Grundfest Schoepf, Harmondsworth, 1997). I have referred above to the role played by Claude Lévi-Strauss.

11 The first results have now been published: Marcel Detienne (ed.), *Qui veut prendre la parole?* Foreword by Pierre Rosanvallon, Paris, 'Le Genre humain' collection, 2003. See chap. VI, pp. 101–25.

12 On the present state of this subject: *Annuaire de l'Ecole pratique des hautes études*, vol. XCIX (1990–1991), Paris, 1992, pp. 243–6. Since then *Apollon, le couteau à la main*, Paris, 1998, has been published.

13 Michel Foucault, *L'Ordre du discours*, Paris, 1971, pp. 16–18.

14 Hesiod, *Theogony*, LL. 27–8 (*ethelein*); *Homeric Hymn to Hermes*, ll. 558–63 (*ethelein*).

15 The herald's formula: Euripides, *Suppliant Women*, 438–9 (*thelein*; the formula of stones designed to be read and visible (*boulesthai*), see Marcel Detienne, 'L'Ecriture et ses nouveaux objects intellectuels en Grèce', in Marcel Detienne (ed.), *Les Savoirs de l'écriture en Grèce ancienne*, Lille, 1992 (1988), p. 41.

16 Marcel Detienne, 'La phalange: problèmes et controverses', in Jean-Pierre Vernant (ed.), *Problèmes de la guerre en Grèce ancienne*, Paris, 1985 (1968), pp. 119–42. In fact, the debate still continues, for warfare and warrior practices are deeply intertwined with the practices of citizenship and political configurations. For recent studies and contrasting points of view, see A. M. Snodgrass, 'The "Hoplite Reform" revisited', *Dialogues d'histoire ancienne*, 19, 1, 1993, pp. 47–61; Hans Van Wees, 'Greeks bearing arms', in Nick Fisher and Hans Van Wees (eds), *Archaic Greece: New Approaches and New Evidence*, London, 1998, pp. 333–78; Moshe Berent, 'Anthropology and the Classics: War, Violence, and the Stateless Polis', *Classical Quarterly*, 50, 1, 2000, pp. 257–89; Peter Krentz, 'Fighting by the Rules. The Invention of the Hoplite Agôn', *Hesperia*, 71, 2002, pp. 23–9.

17 The historian of France as a 'priest of the nation', as he appears in Pierre Nora's semi-historical, semi-narcissistic work, *Lieux de mémoire*, 1984–1992, 7 vols, Paris. Remarkably, in an issue of *Le Débat* (no. 78, 1994), comparison with other European nations prompts Pierre Nora to detect in France 'a historical predisposition toward memories' (pp. 187–91). The French are the *chosen people* where memory and commemoration are concerned: yet again, this derails any comparative approach that demands, first and foremost, a critical analysis of the 'categories' that are involved. The most pertinent remarks on 'a so very French' undertaking have come from outside, either from a sociological viewpoint or from the United

States : J. P. Willaime, ' "Lieux de mémoire" et imaginaire national', *Archives des sciences sociales des religions*, 1988, LXVI, pp. 125–45; S. Englund, in *Journal of Modern History*, 64, 1992, pp. 299–320.

18 Among other studies of a programmatic and polemical nature, see especially Jean Bollack, 'Réflexions sur la pratique philologique', *Informations sur les sciences sociales*, XVI, 3–4, 1976, pp. 375–84.

19 I am thinking of Pierre Judet de la Combe, who generously included *Les Savoirs de l'Ecriture. En Grèce ancienne* in the 'L'apparat critique' collection, under the direction of Jean Bollack. I am particularly grateful as I had presented my thoughts on 'The gods of writing' in the course of the Townsend lectures (February–April 1976) at Cornell University, before an audience that was apparently deeply convinced that the sole god of writing was a French philosopher, Jacques Derrida. The inventions of Palamedes, the Egyptian stories of Thoth and the pronouncements of Orphic writers on letters, *grammata*, were consequently considered meaningless and dismissed. In a future book that I shall surely write one day, I shall endeavour to understand why the stories of 'Mr Palamedes' seemed so incongruous to an audience to which the revelation of Arch-Writing had been vouchsafed. A preliminary study of mythical and intellectual representations of inventive writing appears in two chapters of *The Writing of Orpheus*, translated by Janet Lloyd, Baltimore, 2003, pp. 125–51.

20 The 'Rencontre internationale Hésiode. Philologie. Anthropologie. Philosophie' Colloquium (12–14 October, 1989). The volume entitled *Le Métier du mythe. Lectures d'Hésiode*, edited by F. Blaise, P. Judet de la Combe and P. Rousseau was published by the Presses Universitaires du Septentrion, Lille, in 1996.

21 Three 'roneoed' texts mark out the approach adopted by Heinz Wismann (1976, the Jean Bollack seminar; 1989, the document produced by the Hesiod colloquium; 1993, 'Propositions pour une lecture d'Hésiode'). I shall refer to them by the years in which they appeared.

22 Heinz Wismann, 1993, p. 3.

23 See Andrew Ford, Homer: *The Poetry of the Past*, Ithaca and London, 1992, who demonstrates the complexity of the poetics of the Homeric epic.

24 Heinz Wismann, 1989, p. 5. The parentheses and comments are mine.

25 Heinz Wismann, 1976, p. 5, spoke of 'the immediate transparency of the meaning'. In the 1989 paper, p. 6, he describes *aletheia* as 'the

level of true comprehension' or (p. 7) 'the symbolism of the structure', 'the structures that the auto-reflection of the account make it
possible to grasp'. In Heinz Wismann, 1993, p. 7, all that remains is
the work itself (the *Theogony*), which deploys 'true meanings that
philosophy will continue to study in order to discover its systems'.

26 *Homeric Hymn to Hermes*, lines 558–63.
27 A philologist is recognizable from afar by his/her strained neck,
slightly twisted by the direction of his/her attention, upstream,
towards some previous work or earlier author. With the past before
him he/she has to walk backward.
28 *Iliad*, I, 70.
29 Between 1976 and 1993, not the slightest allusion was made to the
scope of thought on 'Truth-Memory-Forgetfulness' that I had
detected in my 1965 enquiries; whereas completely humdrum
philological studies such as those by H. J. Mette and T. Krischer were
considered worth attention and discussion. Of course such tactics
are not unrelated to strategies adopted to promote 'the philologist's
profession'.
30 Heinz Wismann, 1989, p. 6. In 1993, p. 6, this same hermeneutist
merely alluded to 'the regulatory principle of memory' (?), so
Mnemosyne was stamped into the privative alpha of *alètheia*. In his
work on 'Authority and author in Hesiod's *Theogony*' (Hesiod colloquium, op. cit., p. 13, n. 1), Gregory Nagy produced a critique of the
interpretation proposed by T. Cole, 'Archaic Truth', *Quaderni
Urbinati di Cultura Classica*, 1983, pp. 7–28. While again stressing
the essential relations between 'memory' and 'truth' in poetic
thought ('Authority and author', p. 35), Gregory Nagy tries to show
that the Hesiodic expression *aletheia gerusasthai* refers to a pan-
Hellenic collection of myths that are considered to be radically different from the ever-conflicting local versions.
31 Heinz Wismann, 1989, p. 10.
32 Hesiod, *Theogony*, 4.
33 Id., ibid., 31, followed in line 32 by 'so that I', Hesiod, inspired by
them, 'can sing of what will be and what has been', in other words
in the manner of a diviner and with the speech of diviners (in 31
thespis occurs alongside *aoidè*).
34 The power of the Muses means the power of speech. As early as
1967, Hellenists such as Gregory Nagy and Charles Segal accepted
that the Muses, as the powers of sung speech whose specific names
develop a theology of song with words, represent an essential aspect
of auto-reflection on speech and language. This is something that

hermeneutic knowledge – that of Heinz Wismann, at any rate – seems, literally, to discover, unprompted by any encouragement apart from that which is conveyed by *the words themselves* (?).

35 Hesiod, *Theogony*, ll. 211–32. *Thanatos* and *Hypnos*, L. 212; *Momos*, Blame, at l. 215; *Apate*, Deceit, at L. 224; *Pseudeis Logoi*, Words of deceit, at l. 229. As I have already stressed, Hermes reigns over *Pseudea* just as he does over *haimulioi logoi*, a fact that directly concerns both Pandora and speech exchanged between men and gods.

36 For Gregory Nagy, first in *The Best of the Achaeans*, Baltimore, 1979, *passim* and later in *Pindar's Homer. The Lyric Possession of an Epic Past*, Baltimore, 1990, *passim*.

37 The Derveni Papyrus was discovered in 1962 and presented by S. G. Kapsomenos in 1964, then 'edited' or rather pirated by M. L. West (*ZPE*, XLVII, 1982, '1–12' but without pagination) amid general impatience for the eventual appearance of an edition containing these discoveries. In 1993, the Derveni Papyrus was the subject of an international colloquium in Princeton. See André Laks and Glenn W. Most (eds), *Studies on the Derveni Papyrus*, Oxford, 1997.

38 G. Pugliese-Carratelli, *La Parola del passato*, XXIX, 1974, pp. 108–26.

39 K. Tsantsonoglou, G. M. Parassoglou, 'Two Gold Lamellae from Thessaly', *Hellenika*, XXXVII, 1987, pp. 3–17.

40 See the analyses by F. Graf, 'Textes orphiques et rituel bacchique. A propos des lamelles de Pélinna', in P. Borgeaud (ed.), *Orphisme et Orphée*, Geneva, 1991, pp. 87–102. On the specificity of the choice of writing and books in the Orphic movement, see Marcel Detienne, *The Writing of Orpheus*, translated by Janet Lloyd, Baltimore, 2003, pp. 126–64.

41 M. L. West, 'The Orphics of Olbia', *ZPE*, XLV, 1982, pp. 17–29.

42 For a good guide to the paths and tracks of *Aletheia* according to Heidegger, see M. Zarader, *Heidegger et les paroles de l'origine*, Paris, 2nd (revised) edn, 1990, pp. 49–82.

43 See A. Doz, 'Heidegger, Aristote et le thème de la vérité', *Revue de philosophie ancienne*, I, 1990, pp. 75–96 (in particular, p. 96).

44 Usefully pointed out by A. Doz, ibid., p. 76.

45 See Martin Heidegger, *Introduction à la métaphysique*, translated by G. Kahn, Paris, 1958, pp. 165–7; see also Martin Heidegger, *Gesamtausgabe*, LIII, 1984, p. 100; see pp. 98–9. Interpreters of Heidegger tell us that the construction of words and purely linguistic matters were not what interested him most. Heidegger was determined to illuminate what the Greeks did not clearly perceive: for example, the fact that 'occultation entirely rules the essence of being'.

Was he out to unveil what was veiled? Why not? Clarify things and bring them out into the open? Those certainly were preoccupations of Heidegger and of his poetic and philosophical thinking about Being. *But the Greeks are simply hostages here.* However, even if one thinks that Heidegger is trying to clarify 'the basis for their [the Greeks!] speech and thinking', as Zarader [note 42] does, op. cit., p. 82, this is an interpretation which, like every other interpretation, should face up to objections, admit its shortcomings, and discuss theories developed from other points of view. There can be no 'masters of Truth' where no demonstration is 'geometric'.

46 Moreover, it is claimed that neither Plato nor Aristotle examined the essence of the *polis* (*Gesamtausgabe*, LIII, 1984, p. 99). Who is in the right? The devotees certainly seem to be slipping . . .

47 Open debate is finally possible, with texts at the ready, thanks to the work cited below, note 48, which I have reviewed both in France and in Italy and which I mention in my Preface entitled 'Towards doing anthropology with the Greeks' in the new edition of A. Bonnard, *Civilisation grecque*, vol. I, Brussels, 1991, pp. vii–xiv. All to no avail: no response at all.

48 D. Janicaud, *L'Ombre de cette pensée. Heidegger et la question politique*, Grenoble, 1990.

49 A. Momigliano, *Rivista storica italiana*, XCIV, 3, 1982, pp. 784–7; *Ottavo contributo alla storia degli studi classici e del mondo antico*, Rome, 1987, pp. 381–4.

50 See *The Gardens of Adonis*, translated by Janet Lloyd, Princeton, Mythos collection (Bollinger series), 1994.

51 *Sciences et Avenir*, January 1982, pp. 105–10 ('La mythologie change de sens': an interview with J.-P. Vernant, conducted by H. de Saint Blanquat).

52 That was not exactly the case when, in 1974–5, in my seminars for the ex-VIth section, Hautes Études, I was embarking on a historiographical and *critical* analysis of ancient and contemporary representations of 'myth' and 'mythology'.

53 L. Gernet, *Anthropologie de la Grèce antique*, Paris, 1968, pp. 124, 131, 134, and 185.

54 E. Cassirer, *Philosophie der symbolischen Formen*, vol. 2, *Der mythische Denken*, Hamburg, 1924 (English translation, New Haven, Connecticut 1953).

55 See J.-P. Vernant, *Myth and Thought among the Greeks*, London, Routledge & Kegan Paul, 1983, in particular 'From Myth to Reason', pp. 341–66.

56 Analyses that I presented at Claude Lévi-Strauss's seminar in 1970 and published, initially under the title 'La cuisine de Pythagore', *Archives de sociologie des religions*, XXIX, 1970, pp. 141–62.

57 Those that I pursued for over three years (EPHE, VIth section, 1969–72) in connection with bees, honey, Orion and Orpheus, although all that I have so far published is a paper entitled 'Orphée au miel', in J. Le Goff and P. Nora (eds), *Faire de l'histoire*, vol. III, Paris, 1974, pp. 56–75.

58 See 'Afterword. Revisiting the Gardens of Adonis', *The Gardens of Adonis*, op. cit., pp. 133–45.

59 See the seminars on *Themis* summarized in *L'Annuaire de l'Ecole pratique des hautes études, sciences religieuses*, vol. XCIX (1990–91), Paris, 1992, pp. 243–6.

60 As I. Meyerson stated, years ago, in a review of '*Les Maîtres de vérité dans la Grèce archaïque*', *Journal de psychologie normale et pathologique*, 1970, pp. 225–7.

61 Two approaches to Parmenides, Fr. 7, 5–6: D. Furley, 'Truth as What Survives the Elenchos: an idea of Parmenides', in P. Huby and G. Neal (eds), *The Criterion of Truth*, Liverpool, 1989, pp. 1–2; N. L. Cordero, 'La Déesse de Parménide, maîtresse de philosophie', in J.-F. Mattei (ed.), *La Naissance de la raison en Grèce*, Paris, 1990, pp. 207–14.

62 See M. Detienne (ed.), *Transcrire les mythologies*, Paris, 1994, in particular, the 'opening' (pp. 7–21) and my analyses, 'Manières grecques de commencer' (pp. 159–66).

63 Maurice Caveing, 'La laïcisation de la parole et l'exigence rationnelle', *Raison présente*, January 1969, pp. 95–8.

64 A formula used for 'la cité grecque' between Gernet and Vernant.

65 What I have in mind here are pp. 104–6 at the end of the chapter entitled 'The process of secularization', in *The Masters of Truth in Archaic Greece*, New York, 1996.

66 In the enquiry into writing and its new intellectual subjects, I have already made the following point: while the writing of laws shaped the public space and the field of politics, it was intellectuals – philosophers, doctors, astronomers, geometricians – who, spurred on by *graphein*, introduced entirely new subjects that further opened up paths for thought to follow. See M. Detienne, 'L'Ecriture et ses nouveaux objets intellectuels en Grèce', in M. Detienne, (ed.), *Les Savoirs de l'écriture. En Grèce ancienne*, Lille (1988), 1994, pp. 7–26.

67 Geoffrey Lloyd, *Demystifying Mentalities*, Cambridge, 1990 (translated into French with the title *Pour en finir avec les mentalités*, Paris, 1993). This is an innovative and richly satisfying book on comparison

between different modes of reasoning, beginning with an important enquiry into types of proof, verification and argumentation between different areas of knowledge. A subtly different version of the present chapter has appeared in the new French edition (Pocket-Agora) of *Les Maîtres de vérité dans là Grèce archaïque*. Here, now, is a list of the works that have appeared in the wake of questions raised by the already comparativist genealogical enquiry into 'Truth':

Two analyses of *The Masters of Truth* deserve to be noted:
Caveing, Maurice, 'La laïcisation de la parole et l'exigence rationelle', *Raison présente*, January 1969, pp. 85–98
Croissant, Jeanne, 'Sur quelques problèmes d'interprétation en histoire de la philosophie grecque', *Revue de l'Université de Bruxelles*, 1973, 3–4, pp. 376–91.

On what is to be made of 'mythical thought'?:
Detienne, Marcel, *L'Invention de la mythologie*, Paris, Gallimard, 1987 (revised edition, 1991). 'Revisiting the Gardens of Adonis', Afterword, in *The Gardens of Adonis. Spices in Greek Mythology*, Princeton 1994, revised and corrected edition, pp. 133–48.
Veyne, Paul, *Les Grecs ont-ils cru à leurs mythes? Essai sur l'imagination constituante*, Paris, 1983 (*Did the Greeks Believe in Their Myths? An Essay on the Constitutive Imagination*, Chicago, 1988).

On religious thought, configurations of rationality, thought and society:
Lloyd, G. E. R. *Magic, Reason and Experience. Studies in the origins and development of Greek Science*, Cambridge, 1979
— *The Revolutions of Wisdom. Studies in the Claims and Practice of Ancient Greek Science*, Berkeley and Los Angeles, 1987
Mattei, Jean-François (ed.), *La Naissance de la raison en Grèce*, Paris, 1990
Vernant, Jean-Pierre, *Myth and Thought among the Greeks*, London, 1983.

On memory, the Muses and truth:
Simondon, Michèle, *La Mémoire et l'oubli dans la pensée grecque jusqu'à la fin du Ve siècle av. J.-C.*, Paris, 1982.

On a number of notions and categories the institutional meaning of which affect my enquiry into the 'Masters of Truth':

Benveniste, Emile, *Le Vocabulaire des institutions indo-européennes*, I–II, Paris, 1969.

On cunning, deceit, seduction and persuasion:
Detienne, Marcel and Vernant, Jean-Pierre, *Cunning Intelligence in Greek Culture and Society*, translated by Janet Lloyd, Hassocks, Sussex, 1978.

On problems concerning speech:
Leclerc, Marie-Christine, *La Parole chez Hésiode*, Paris, 1993
Svenbro, Jesper, *La Parola e il marmo. Alle origini della poetica greca*, Turin, 1984.

On 'the part played by truth' in historical enquiry:
Darbo-Peschanski, Catherine, *Le Discours du particulier. Essai sur l'enquête hérodotéenne*, Paris, 1987.

On divination and truth:
Couloubaritsis, Lambros, 'L'Art divinatoire et la question de la vérité', *Kernos*, 3, 1990, pp. 113–22
Sauge, André, *De l'Epopée à l'histoire. Fondements de la notion de l'histoire*, Frankfurt, 1992

On writing, democracy, public space and new learning:
Detienne, Marcel (ed.), *Les Savoirs de l'écriture. En Grèce ancienne*, Lille, 1994 (1st edn, 1988).

More specifically on the semantic field of *muthos* in Homeric epic:
Martin, Richard P., *The Language of Heroes*, Ithaca-London, 1989.

On interpretations of Parmenides:
Cordero, Nestor-Luis, *Les Deux chemins de Parménide*, Paris-Brussels, 1984
Couloubaritsis, Lambros, *Mythe et philosophie chez Parménide*, Brussels, 1990 (1st edn, 1986)
Pierre Aubenque (ed.), *Etudes sur Parménide*, I–II, Paris, 1987 (the first volume and the translation of Parmenides' poem and the critical essay are by Denis O'Brien in collaboration with Jean Frère)
Parménides. Sur la nature ou sur l'étant, introduction, translation and commentary by Barbara Cassin, Paris, 1998.

On *Aletheia*, its original essence, developments of the interpretation constructed by Heidegger and on ancient paradigms, two contrasting approaches:

Cassin, Barbara, 'Grecs et Romains. Les paradigmes de l'antiquité chez Arendt et Heidegger', in H. Arendt, *Ontologie et politique*, Paris, 1989

Zarader, Marlène, *Heidegger et les paroles de l'origine*, Paris, 2nd edn (revised), 1990.

On *Aletheia* and *alethes*, semantic analyses and philological readings by:

Cole, Thomas, 'Archaic Truth', *Quaderni Urbinati di Cultura Classica*, 1983, pp. 7–28 (with critical remarks by G. Nagy, 'Autorité et auteur dans la *Théogonie* hésiodique', in *Le Métier du mythe. Lectures d'Hésiode*, op. cit.)

Huby, P. and Neal, G. (eds), *The Criterion of Truth*, Liverpool 1989

Levet, Jean-Pierre, *Le Vrai et le faux dans la pensée grecque archaïque. Etude de vocabulaire*, vol. I, Paris, 1976

Snell, Bruno, *Der Weg zum Denken und zur Wahrheit (Hypomnemata*, vol. 57), 1978, pp. 91–104.

Two books of a more general nature:

Balibar, Etienne, *Lieux et noms de la vérité*, Paris, 1994

Hénaff, Marcel, *Le Prix de la vérité: le don, l'argent, la philosophie*, Paris, 2002.

Chapter 5 'Digging In'

1 For the sake of brevity, on questions arising from autochthony, I refer the reader to my little treatise, *Comment être autochtone. Du pur Athénien au Français raciné*, Paris, 2003, in particular the chapter entitled 'Une autochtonie d'immaculée conception, nos Athéniens', pp. 19–59.

2 In Alain Rey (ed.), *Le Robert. Dictionnaire historique de la langue française*, Paris, 1998.

3 These questions are raised in an earlier volume of comparative studies by ethnologists and historians working in collaboration: Marcel Detienne (ed.), *Tracés de fondation*, Bibl. Ecole des hautes études, Sciences religieuses, vol. CXIII, Louvain-Paris, 1990.

4 I tackled this question earlier, in Giulia Sissa and Marcel Detienne, 'The Power of Women: Hera, Athena, and their Followers', *The Daily Life of the Greek Gods*, translated by Janet Lloyd, Stanford, 2000, pp. 208–29; and I returned to it in 'L'Art de fonder l'autochtonie. Entre Thèbes, Athènes et le Français de souche', *Vingtième siècle. Revue d'histoire*, 69, 2001, pp. 105–10.

5 See the fascinating analysis of Australia facing up to its colonial past in Isabelle Merle, 'Le Mabo Case', *Annales HSS*, 1998, no. 2, pp. 209–29.

6 See Nicole Loraux's in-depth analysis, *The Invention of Athens. The Funeral Oration in the Classical City*, translated by Alan Sheridan, London and Cambridge, Mass., 1986.

7 Aspasia of Miletus in Plato's rendering of her 'Funeral Oration': 'Our city is imbued with a whole-hearted hatred of alien races' (Plato, *Menexenus*, 245d).

8 See *Comment être autochtone*, op. cit., p. 53.

9 See note 4.

10 See *Comment être autochtone*, op. cit., p. 166, n. 71. It is worth noting once again that so far there is no hint of any defilement provoked by *incest* of any kind, although Oedipus did, of course, shed his father's blood and *'plough his furrow'*. A remark in passing on Oedipus: so far from being a 'scapegoat' is he that, in *The Phoenician Women* (admittedly according not to Freud but to Euripides), Jocasta tells us, the spectators, that poor Oedipus has been confined to house arrest by his wicked sons.

11 Details and further comments may be found in *Comment être autochtone*, op. cit., pp. 61–120.

12 Consider, for example, how ethnic integration proceeds in Britain: Verena Stolcke, 'Europe: nouvelles frontières, nouvelles rhétoriques de l'exclusion', in Daniel Fabre (ed.), *L'Europe entre cultures et nations*, Paris, 1996, pp. 227–55.

13 Helped by anthropologists such as Frank Salomon and Stuart B. Schwartz (eds), *The Cambridge History of the Native Peoples of the Americas*, vol. III, Cambridge, 1999, vols. I and II.

14 Presented in Marcel Detienne, *Comparer l'incomparable*, Paris, 2000, p. 46, in which I stress the role that Charles Malamoud has played in reflection upon 'What is a place?'.

15 An enquiry the nature of which is indicated by the subtitle, *Du pur Athénien au français raciné*, of the work cited in note 1.

16 See Marta Machiavelli, 'La Ligue du Nord et l'invention du "Padan" ', *Critique internationale*, no. 10, 2001, pp. 129–42.

17 Marta Machiavelli, op. cit., p. 141, who remarks upon this 'theory' that is defended by Gilberto Oneto, *L'Invenzione della Padania*, Bergamo, 1990, on the extreme right of the Northern League.

18 See Jean-François Gossiaux, *Pouvoirs ethniques dans les Balkans*, Paris, 2002, pp. 133–88.

19 Maurice Barrès, *Scènes et doctrines du nationalisme*, Paris, 1925, I, p. 118, together with a touch of 'Grandeur du français raciné', in *Comment être autochtone*, op. cit., pp. 123–49.

20 This is a line of enquiry opened up by Gérard Noiriel, *La Tyrannie du national. Le droit d'asile en Europe*, Paris, 1991, and also in a series of new and courageous articles: 'La question nationale comme objet d'histoire sociale', *Genèses*, 4, 1991, pp. 72–94; 'L'Identité nationale dans l'historiographie française. Note sur un problème', in Jacques Chevallier (ed.), *L'Identité politique*, Paris, 1994, pp. 294–305.

21 Mirko Grmek, Marc Gjidara and Neven Simac, *Le nettoyage ethnique. Documents historiques sur une idéologie serbe* (1993), Paris, 2002. Also Alice Krieg-Planque, *'Purification ethnique'. Une formule et son histoire*, Paris, 2003.

22. Fernand Braudel, *L'Identité de France* (1986, 3 vols), Paris, (in a single volume, 'Mille et une pages' coll.), 1990, p. 10.

23 Along with Alphonse Dupront, he is honoured in the chapter entitled 'Grandeur du français raciné' in *Comment être autochtone*, op. cit., pp. 121–49.

24 All the references required by students and readers eager to know more may be found in op. cit., pp. 121–49.

25 A point drawn to my attention by Milad Doueihi, who took part in a comparativist seminar on 'Dénationaliser les histoires nationales' held partly in Johns Hopkins University, Baltimore, USA, and partly in Paris.

26 A project suggested in *Comparer l'incomparable*, Paris, 2000, pp. 61–80 and undertaken with the support of Gérard Lenclud and François Hartog.

27 *Discours de réception de Pierre Nora à l'Académie française et réponse de René Rémond* . . ., Paris, 2002, pp. 70 and 73.

28 Jacques Revel and André Burguière (eds), *Histoire de la France* (1989), Paris, 2000, I ('L'Espace français'), pp. 11–12.

29 Op. cit., p. 8. It would appear that, to date, nothing has changed since the 1950s either in Italy or in Germany, Spain or any other part of Europe. In this thinking on one (only one?) 'crisis of historical identity', the only subject addressed is 'us', 'we French', together

with all the little dramas in 'our' history. Any exclusively national history that, today as yesterday (op. cit., pp. 28–9), wonders what its best 'exportable' product might be is surely pathetic. Barrès held that 'nationalism' meant resolving every problem that arose in relation to France. Well, bravo, Barrès . . . .

30   Op. cit., p. 21 (my italics).
31   See Fernand Braudel, op. cit., p. 389.
32   Jacques Revel and André Burguière, op. cit., p. 17.
33   Christopher Hughes, *Switzerland*, New York, 1975; Olivier Zimmer, 'Competing Memories of the Nation: liberal historians and the reconstruction of the Swiss past, 1870–1900', *Past and Present*, no. 168, 2001, pp. 194–226.
34   Jean-Christoph Attias and Esther Benbassa, *Israël, la terre et le sacré*, 2nd edn, Paris, 2001.
35   Whether or not you are 'pedigree' French, see, as a matter of urgency, Gérard Noiriel, *Les Origines républicaines de Vichy*, Paris, 1999, in particular pp. 211–72 ('Savants, experts et pouvoir d'Etat'). I wonder when we can expect to find a chapter on 'historians' who are, after all, also scholars and experts.
36   See and spread the news of the excellent essay by Amin Maalouf, *Les Identités meurtrières*, Paris, 1998.

Chapter 6   Comparabilities

1   I have already argued in favour of such ideas and written to defend them in Marcel Detienne, *Comparer l'incomparable*, Paris, 2000, pp. 105–27; Marcel Detienne (ed.), *Qui veut prendre la parole?*, Paris, 2003 ('Des pratiques d'assemblée aux formes du politique', pp. 13–30; 'Retour sur comparer et arrêt sur comparables', pp. 415–28).
2   See the works of Iaroslav Lebedynsky, cited in his 'Les Cosaques, rites et métamorphoses d'une *démocratie guerrière*', in *Qui veut prendre la parole?*, op. cit., pp. 147–70.
3   Marc Abélès has played an important role in these comparative studies, first with his *Le Lieu du politique*, Paris, 1983, and then with his 'Revenir chez les Ochollo', in *Qui veut prendre la parole?* op. cit., pp. 393–413.
4   A book of major importance for a re-examination of Greek cities is: Françoise Ruzé, *Délibération et pouvoir dans la cité grecque. De Nestor à Socrate*, Paris, 1997. See also her contribution, 'Des cités grecques:

en guerre et en délibération', in *Qui veut prendre la parole?*, op. cit.,
pp. 171–89.

5 See Marcel Detienne (ed.), *Qui veut prendre la parole?*, op. cit., an
   enquiry that I initiated in Marseilles, where I encountered my first
   problems (pp. 417–18), and later completed in a 'colloquial' phase,
   in Paris, at the Fondation des Sciences Politiques (in 2000).

6 'Collective' works – all of them, whether they have been rethought
   or have simply been rescued from the back of some drawer – are
   unlikely to be widely circulated except to university libraries. I
   therefore have no hesitation at all in repeating, in this chapter, the
   questions and problems that have already been discussed in *Qui veut
   prendre la parole?*. I do so in order to reach those who would like to
   know more and think more about them. In every instance I shall cite
   the title of the work in which these contributions have already
   appeared.

7 On Philippe-Joseph Salazar, 'En Afrique du Sud. Eloges démocra-
   tiques', op. cit., pp. 33–45.

8 See Jean-Philippe Heurtin, 'Architectures morales de l'Assemblée
   nationale', op. cit., pp. 49–81.

9 See Pierre-François Souyri, 'Des communautés monastiques dans le
   Japon médiéval', op. cit., pp. 85–94; Hélène Millet, 'Chanoines
   séculiers et conseils de prélats. En France, à la fin du Moyen Age', op.
   cit., pp. 95–106; Andras Zempléni, 'Les assemblées secrètes du Poro
   Sénoufo (Nafara, Côte d'Ivoire)', op. cit., pp. 107–44.

10 See Iaroslav Lebedynsky, 'Les Cosaques, rites et métamorphoses
   d'une *démocratie guerrière*', op. cit., pp. 147–70; Françoise Ruzé, 'Des
   cités grecques: en guerre et en délibération', op. cit., pp. 171–90;
   Georges Charachidzé, 'En Circassie: comment s'occuper du gou-
   vernement des hommes', op. cit., pp. 191–210.

11 See Jean-Pierre Delumeau, 'De l'assemblée précommunale au
   temps des conseils. En Italie centrale', op. cit., pp. 213–28;
   Gabriella Rossetti, 'Entre Pise et Milan', op. cit., pp. 229–42;
   Odilon Redon, 'Parole, témoignage, décision dans les assemblées
   communales en Toscane méridionale aux XII–XIIIe siècles', op.
   cit., pp. 243–55.

12 See Jean-Marie Durand, ' "Se réunir" en Syrie. Au temps du
   royaume de Mari', op. cit., pp. 259–72; Yves Schemeil, 'Entre le
   Tigre et le Nil, hier et aujourd'hui', op. cit., pp. 273–302; Jean-Paul
   Latouche, 'Maison d'assemblée au milieu du Pacifique', op. cit.,
   pp. 303–25.

13   See Jacques Guilhaumou, 'Un argument saisi dans le mouvement démocratique, la souveraineté délibérante, à Marseille', op. cit., pp. 329–48; Sophie Wahnich, 'Recevoir et traduire la voix du peuple', op. cit., pp. 349–72; Patrick Brasart, 'Des Commons au Manège: effets d'écho en Chambre sourde', op. cit., pp. 373–89.

14   See Marc Abélès, 'Revenir chez les Ochollo', op. cit., pp. 393–413.

15   See 'Les vertus d'un comparatisme dérangeant', Pierre Rosanvallon's Foreword to *Qui veut prendre la parole?*, op. cit., pp. 7–12.

Names and General Index

Names Index

Abélès, Marc 102, 150(n3), 152(n14)
Académie française 92
Aeschylus 76–7
Anacreon of Samos 30
Assurbanipal 45
Athena 80–1
Attias, Jean-Christophe 109, 150(n34)
Aubenque, Pierre 146

Barrès, Maurice 6, 92, 96, 149(n19)
Benbassa, Esther 109, 150(n34)
Bertillon, Alphonse 88
Bodeü, Richard 131
Bonte, Pierre 131(n4)
Bopp, Franz 18
Brassart, Patrick 152(n13)
Braudel, Fernand 6, 91, 90–2, 93, 94–5,
    149(n22), 150(n31)
Burguière, André 93–4, 99, 149(n28,
    n29), 150(n32)

Cadmus 77, 81
Cain 48
Calchas 67
Cassirer, Ernst 22–3, 24, 26, 27, 28, 63,
    72, 143(n54)
Caveing, Maurice 75, 144(n63), 145
Charachidzé, Georges 151(n10)
Cole, Thomas 147
Croissant, Jeanne 145

Daedalus 31
Darbo-Peschanski, Catherine
    146

Decharme, Paul 20
Delumeau, Jean-Pierre 151(n11)
Derrida, Jacques 140(n19)
Detienne, Marcel 131(n8), 132(n12,
    n17, n18), 134(n), 136(n1, n4, n10)
    137(n18), 138(n25), 139(n11n
    n15, n16), 142(n49), 144(n62,
    n66), 145, 146, 147(n3, n4),
    148(n14), 150(n1), 151(n5)
Donato, Ricardo Di 63
Doueihi, Milad 149(n25)
Dumézil, Georges 34, 55, 133(n27),
    137(n20)
Dupront, Alphonse 149(n23)
Durand, Jean-Marie 151(n12)
Durkheim, Emile 4, 6, 23–4, 26–7, 72,
    86, 131(n9, n10)

Elias, Norbert 85–6
Epimenides 61
Erechtheus 80–1

Fisher, Nick 139
Fontenelle, Bernard le Bovier de 8,
    16–17, 20
Foucault, Michel 62, 64, 138(n4),
    139(n13)
Frazer, James George 3–4, 25
Fustel de Coulange 127

Gernet, Louis 25–6, 63, 72, 134(n),
    138(n6), 143(n53), 144(n64)
Granet, Marcel 25
Grmek, Mirko 149(n21)

Heidegger, Martin 69–71, 142–3(n42, n45), 146
Hera 68
Herodotus 30, 31, 32, 52, 82
Hesiod 16, 30, 39, 41, 61, 64, 65, 66, 67, 68, 73, 74, 138(n5), 139(n14), 141(n32, n33), 142(n35)
Hestia 109
Heurtin, Jean-Philippe 151(n7)
Hitler, Adolf 71

Ise 54
Izard, Michel 131(n4)

Janicaud, Dominique 71, 143(n48)

Karady, V. 131(n9)
Kuhn, Adalbert 20

Lafitau, Joseph-François 8, 16–17, 20
Lang, Andrew 20, 34
Latouché, Jean-Paul 151(n12)
Lavisse, Ernest 6–7, 92, 132(n15)
Le Pen, Jean-Marie 91
Lebedynsky, Iaroslav 150(n2), 151(n10)
Leclerc, Marie-Christine 146
Leenhardt, Maurice 5
Lenclud, Gérard 132(n12), 137(n15), 149(n26)
Le Pen, Jean-Marc 91
Lévi-Strauss, Claude 5, 21–2, 27–9, 34, 35–8, 58–9, 63, 72, 131(n1), 132(n13), 133(n27), 135(n), 136(n2), 137(n21), 138(n10, n26), 143(n56)
Lloyd, Geoffrey 75, 144–5(n67)

Macé, François 41–5, 136(n4)
Machiavelli, Niccolò 106
Malamoud, Charles 148(n14)
Mauss, Marcel 5, 22, 35
Mauzé, Marie 137(n15)
Mégret, Bruno 91
Metis 68
Millet, Hélène 151(n9)
Momigliano, Arnaldo 72, 143(n49)
Morgan, Lewis 6, 132(n14)
Müller, Friedrich-Max 18–19, 20, 28, 34
Müller, Karl Otfried 22–3

Nagy, Gregory 69, 135(n), 141(n30n n34), 142(n36)

Noiriel, Gérard 89, 149(n20), 150(n35)
Nora, Pierre 93, 139(n17), 144(n57)

Oedipus 77, 81–2, 148(n10)
Orpheus 69, 85
Otto, Walter F. 22

Palamedes 140
Parmenides 9, 26, 61, 70, 73, 74, 144
Pindar 30–1
Plato 6, 28, 33–4, 39, 41, 47, 66, 91, 143(n47)
Poseidon 80–1
Praxithea 83

Redon, Odilon 151(n11)
Revel, Jacques 93–4, 99, 149(n28, n29), 150(n32)
Ricoeur, Paul 92, 95
Robichet, Théo 91
Romulus 83
Rosanvallon, Pierre 139(n11), 152(n15)
Rossetti, Gabriella 151(n11)
Ruzé, Françoise 150(n4)

Salazar, Philippe-Joseph 115, 151(n7)
Scheid, John 55, 137(n19)
Schelling, Friedrich Wilhelm Joseph 22
Schemeil, Yves 151(n12)
Schnapper, Dominique 88
Segal, Charles 69, 141(n34)
Selinus 81
Severi, Carlo 52
Souyri, Pierre-François 151(n9)
Spensithius 57–8

Themis 68
Themistocles 80
Thucydides 29, 31, 32–3, 34
Thyades 67
Thoth 140(n19)
Tylor, Edward Burnett 2, 3, 20–2, 26, 28

Valensi, Lucette 133(n28)
Vandermeersch, L. 137(n22), 138(n23, n24)
Vegetti, Mario 136(n10)
Vernant, Jean-Pierre 63, 72, 132(n16), 135, 138(n7), 143(n55), 145, 146

Vesta 109
Vidal-Naquet, Pierre 65

Wismann, Heinz 66–7, 140–1(n21, n22,
n24, n25, n30, n31n 34)

Xenophanes of Colophon 8, 28, 29, 30,
34

Zempléni, Andras 151(n9)

General Index

aboriginal, aborigines 13, 20, 78–9, 96, 97
abstraction 26–7, 74
agora 62–3, 74, 112
Aletheia 60–3, 65, 67, 68, 69, 73, 75,
140(n25)
alphabet 46–7, 57
Americans 15–17
Amerindians 58–9
Ancient Greece 25–6
Ancient World 17
annals, annalists 44, 53–4, 56, 58
anthropologists 2, 27, 84, 103, 126
anthropologos 2
anthropology 1–14, 65, 66, 71, 87, 99,
125, 128–9
comparative 2–3, 5, 6, 7, 10
exotic 128
Greek 4–5, 7
and history 10
limitations 7
origins 2
as Science of Civilization 8
archaeologists 89, 99
archaeology 32–3, 98
assemblies
communal 119–21
comparing beginnings 106–8
Cossack, Greek, Circassian 118–19
English/French 122–3
holding 121–2
justice 110–11
oaths 120
opening/closing 64
places of equality 116–18
practices of 104–6
public matters 108–10
right to join 115
space 115–16
Australia, Australians 8, 78–9
authenticity 128
autochthony 7, 9, 43–4, 44, 76–8,
79–82, 95, 98, 99–100

aboriginal 78–9
Athenian 79–81
being national 83–6
Theban 81–3

Bedouins 99
Bee-Women 64, 67–8
Bushmen 20
Buddhism 54, 109, 114
Bugis-Makassar 49, 50, 52

canons, secular 117
China, ancient 44–5, 56–7
Circassians 106, 118–19, 124
cities 33–4, 47, 49, 58, 74, 102
citizenship 87, 110, 111, 112–13, 114,
117, 120
active 112
centred on fixed space 112–13
civilization 1, 5, 6, 7, 20, 51
colonization 84
comparativism 5, 6–13, 66, 73–4, 75,
82, 124–5, 127–30
concept 6
dissonances 12, 13
experimental/constructive 10, 12–13,
99–100
founding/establishing a territory
12–14
intellectual/civic virtues 92–5
methodology 10
political 101
in practice 95–7
practice of beginnings 106–8
as profession 11–12
types of 3
comparabilities 101–25
Constituent Assembly 103, 106, 107,
116, 122–3
Cossacks 103, 106, 107, 109, 111,
113–14, 118–19
creator-gods 48–9

Crete 57–8, 61
cult practices 16
cultural competence 39–40
culture 1, 2, 6, 23, 37, 87
  biblical 47
  discovering 12–13
  Greek 75
  oral 53
  primitive/savage societies 5
  Protestant 43
  rooted in mythical thought 24
  sociology of 65
  transmission of 50
  variability of 49, 129
Cuna people 52

the dead 92, 94–5, 97
Delphic oracle 58
democracy 8, 9, 101–2, 103, 117, 124
digging in 76–100
dissonances 12

Egypt 126
Englishness 90
enquirers 41
Epimenides 61
equality 109, 110, 111
  places of 116–18
  sameness-equality 113–15
  theoretical 114
Ethiopian communities 64, 102–3, 123–4
Ethnic cleansing 190
ethnography 99
ethnologists 10–14, 50, 58–9, 117, 129
ethnology 5, 10, 92, 126–7
etymology 70–1
experimentation 10, 12–13, 64, 85, 99–100, 102, 127, 129

fables 16–17, 20, 26, 32, 33
faire son trou 76–100
foundation 13, 48, 53, 54, 58, 77, 78
France 4, 6, 44, 84, 85, 88, 91, 93
France,-the-Person 93–4, 99
freedom 1, 84

The Galigo 52
geographers 99
God of Israel 45, 46, 48, 98
Greece 7, 25, 27, 55, 58, 114
Greeks 52, 125, 127–9

  anthropology of 4–5
  appropriation of 7
  as civilized 7, 8
  classification 6, 8
  comparative approach 6, 8
  as initiators 41
  philosophical place of 26–7
  and taste for the universal 60
  time/space thinking 58
  values of 7
  and writing/transcription 42–3, 46–7, 49

hearsay 32, 33
Hellenists 4, 69, 77, 103, 126–8
hermeneutics 65–8
historical research 56
Historical Science 4, 6, 9
historicity 9, 46–57
  comparative 92
  effect of writing on 53
  and God of Israel 45–9
  regimes of 49–52, 53–4
historiography 9, 43, 45, 52, 56, 96
history 6, 65, 92, 125
  communal approach 6
  exclusion of the fabulous 31
  Greek origins 7
  as *historia*/enquiry 9
  and myth of origin 6–7
  national 4, 6–7, 89–91
Holy Land 98
Homeric Hymn to Hermes 67
honey 67–8
hoplite reform 62, 65, 74
House of Commons 101, 122–3
House of Tablets 51

identity 59, 85, 96, 99–100
  myth-ideologies 99–100
  national 9, 86–9, 93
  singular/original 94
  through identification 88
  unique 93, 94
Indonesians 52
intuition 24
Israel 45–6, 47–9, 57, 77, 90, 96, 97–8
Italy 84–5, 93

Japan 42, 44–5, 49, 50, 52, 53–4, 89, 92, 109, 116, 124

Jews 46, 71, 90
  pedigree 97–9
Juda 51
Judaism 45–6, 47–9
justice 7, 110–11, 120
  king of 61, 68

Kanaka 43–4, 52, 59
Kojiki 44, 45, 54
ktizein 58

language 1, 56, 62–3
  conveyance of concepts 25
  dialectical 18
  link with myth 18, 21, 24
  of mythology 34
  mythopoietic 18–19
  primitive 18, 19
  science of 20
  sickness in 19
  as speech of the people 18
  thematic 18
laws 58, 61
Lethe 61, 62, 68
logographers 29, 31, 32, 39, 52
logopoios 52
logos 62–3

Masters of Truth 60–3, 68, 74, 75
mathematics 75
Melanesia 43–4
memory 32, 33, 44, 46, 52, 53, 54, 57,
  61, 66, 73
  communal 38
  daughters of 67
  guardians 50, 51
  mythico-religious 69
  sites 85
Mesopotamia 48, 51, 77, 126
Ministry of Cultural Identity and
  Memory 85
Ministry of Cultural Identity and
  National Consciousness 99
Ministry of National Education 6
Mnemosyne 61–2 68
Monastic communities 116–17
monks 44, 109–10, 114, 115, 116
monotheism 22
morality 28
myth-analysis 34–6
  contexts 36
  field of comparison 37

levels of meaning 37, 38, 39
  recognition of the mythical 38–9
  relationships 36
  structural 37, 39
  transformation 36
myth-ideology 90, 93, 96, 99–100
myth/s 8, 72
  analysis/interpretation of 25–6
  as deceptive/seductive 31
  definitions 21, 23, 28–9, 35
  degradation into history 59
  features of 22
  as forgeries, *plasmata*, pure fictions 30
  as forgotten world 23
  Greek interpretation 29
  as illusory, incredible, stupid 30
  immoral nature of 20
  initial interpretation 29–31
  link with language 18, 21, 24
  move to reason 26–7
  natural phenomena 19
  nature of 8, 15
  as original experience made manifest
    22
  overtaking of 27–9
  power/symbolism 25
  realities of 23
  as religion 24
  removal of concrescence 23
  ritual/transmission 25
  science of 20
  stories told by others 30, 31
mythic consciousness 23–4, 27
mythical data 26
mythical thought 25, 26, 35, 38, 63, 65
  and foundation of anthropology 20–2
  metamorphoses of 71–5
  philosophical/sociological 22–4
mythietai 30
mythographers 39, 43, 52
mythology 8, 65, 90
  attentive reading of 26
  comparative 16, 20–2
  concept 41
  definitions 28, 35
  familiarity with 15
  as framework 39–40
  Greek 30
  language of 34
  as lore 39–40
  mimetic character of 33
  as naive/simple 23

mythology (*cont.*)
  as narrative genre 35–6
  national 7, 92–5, 93
  nature of 15–16
  and patterns of behaviour 26
  philosophical/spiritual view 22
  Platonic city 33–4
  primitive/mythical thought debate 8
  similarities 16
  status of 8
  as system of representation 35
mythos 30–1

narrative 67
nation 4, 55–6, 79, 84, 85, 86, 94, 99
nationalism 83–6, 92, 95
nationality 88, 97, 98, 99
nationhood 4, 7, 86
Native Americans 16, 20
New Caledonia 43–4, 49, 50, 52
New South Wales 78–9
New Testament 51, 66
New World 1, 3, 7, 15–17
Nihonshoki 44, 54

Observers of Mankind 2
Occidentalism 9
Ochollo 102, 103, 106, 124
Office of Historiography 57
Olbia 69, 70
Old Woman 110, 117
oral communication 33
oral tradition 5, 32, 35, 38, 59
oral transmission 38, 50

Padania 84–5
polis 70–1, 112
politics 9, 51, 58, 64, 70–1
  abstract/concrete 103
  assemblies 104–6, 115–24
  comparative beginnings 101–3,
    106–8
  invention of 104
  justice 110–11
  place for 123–4
  places for 103–4
  public matters 108–10
  sameness-equality 108, 113–15
pontifex maximus 55
pontiffs 54–7
positivism 27, 74
primordial peoples 48, 79

proofs, types of 65
Pythagoreanism 61–2

rationalism 72, 75
'Religions of Non-civilized Peoples' 5
'Religions of Peoples Without Writing'
  5–6
rhetoric 63
ritual 25–6, 55, 62, 69, 83, 105
Rome 54–6

sameness 113–15
savage peoples 21–2
scandal 20, 30
science 25
scribes 42, 51–2, 57–8
seers/diviners 56, 61, 67
semiotics 35, 36, 37–8
singular 36
Senoufo 110, 116, 117–18
Serbs 90
Sicily 102, 103, 112
Sima /qian 56
sophistry 63
sovereignty 26, 53, 92, 110, 118–19
space 74, 77, 83
space-time 58, 129
specificity 128
speech 18, 25, 30, 117
  assembly/environment 64
  dialogue 74
  funeral orations 89
  Hesiodic 65–8
  magico-religious 74
  poetic 61, 66
  public 16
  religious/mythical representations 73
  secularization of 62–3, 74
stories 16, 17, 20–1, 30, 31, 32, 38, 42,
  43, 45, 51, 52, 59
storytellers 43
structuralism 35, 37, 66
Sumeria 48
Sumero-Akkadian culture 45
Switzerland 96–7

terra nullius 78–9
territory, territorializing 77
thought, thinking
  ancient 25
  argumentation, non-contradiction,
    dialogue 62

categories 65
changes in 27
local 27
modes of 29
mythical 20–4, 25, 26, 35, 38, 63, 65, 71–5
philosophical/historical combination 34
pre-historical 28
rational 72, 75
scientific 27
secularization of 74
transition 62
time 55–6, 56, 67–8
transcriptions
  Amerindian 58–9
  comparative regimes of historicity 49–52
  Cretan 57–8
  Greek 42–3, 46–7, 49
  Japanese 42, 44–5
  Judaic 45–6, 47–9
  Melanesian 43–4
  reception of tradition 52–7
  results of 41–2

transmission 25, 38, 50
truth 8, 9, 32, 60–75

universal suffrage 87, 88, 89
universitas 119–21
vocabulary 25, 30, 63

Walachia 85
Warriors 62–3, 111, 114, 115, 118–19
will to assemble 104–6, 107, 108, 115
will to knowledge 64
will to truth 64
writing 5–6, 29, 32, 42, 57
  adoption of 50–1
  as cognitive practice 65
  effect of 43, 51–2
  establishment of 44–5
  importance of 69
  knowledge/exploitation of 47
  link with orality 8–9
  nationalist mode 89
  political 47

Zakhor 46